Guerilla Data Analysis
Using Microsoft Excel

Guerilla Data Analysis Using Microsoft Excel
Copyright© 2002 by Bill Jelen

Written by:

Bill Jelen, MrExcel
Visit the MrExcel web site at www.MrExcel.com

Edited by:

Anne Troy & Linda DeLonais

On the Cover:

As if going to war with themselves, a barrage of Excel equations battle it out on the front of the book jacket. Design by Irubin Consulting (www.Irubin.com)

Published by:

Holy Macro! Books
13386 Judy Avenue Northwest
Uniontown, Ohio, USA 44685

Distributed by:

Holy Macro! Books

First printing:

August 2002
Printed in the United States of America

Library of Congress Data

Jelen, Bill
      Guerilla Data Analysis Using Microsoft Excel / Bill Jelen
Library of Congress Control Number: 2002117109
ISBN: 0-9724258-0-2

About the Author

Better known online as "Mr. Excel", Bill Jelen is the brains behind MrExcel.com.

Bill works with clients all over the world, designing custom Excel applications, solving their Excel emergencies and providing tips and hints that help Excel users get the most out of their spreadsheet applications.

Bill Jelen's adventures in spreadsheets began while receiving his B.A. in Management from the University of Notre Dame. Bill was a teaching assistant, responsible for administering the world's most difficult examination in Lotus 1-2-3. After months of grading exams for a research project and never finding an MBA candidate who could score more than about 60%, Bill set out to learn enough about Lotus 1-2-3 to ace the test.

After Notre Dame, Bill joined Telxon Corporation in Akron, Ohio. Over his 15-year career at Telxon, he held a variety of positions. As a Programmer, the applications he developed had an immediate impact on productivity and continued to be used in production for over twelve years – eons, really, in the programming world. Bill was promoted to Financial Systems Analyst. As a team member on a McKinsey & Company Consulting Study, he co-developed an Excel-based analysis model that saved the company $8.6 million in the nine years it was used. Bill also designed a margin analysis that exposed low-margin products, which allowed the company to save over $500,000 annually. In 1996, Bill was promoted to Director of Operations Analysis where he continued on his mission to improve productivity and free management from the tedium of manual data collection and reporting. He developed a pilot system in Excel in one day, launched it the next day, and eventually eliminated a high-level management position that managed the now-obsolete manual process. That application eventually grew to contain 2,400+ lines of VBA code and was managed with a single button click made daily by an administrative assistant.

Bill was awarded two patents while at Telxon; one was for a reversible keyboard for a handheld computer. Long before it was fashionable, Bill invented and patented a system to allow ordering of groceries over the Internet. Unfortunately, his employer took control of the patent in exchange for a fancy catered lunch and a $42 plaque for Bill's office. Now he knows how Al Gore feels.

MrExcel.com was conceived in 1998 with Bill's founding of Tickling Keys, Inc., a Microsoft Excel Consulting and Web Publishing practice. When he first launched MrExcel.com, he had no idea it would rocket to the nearly 10-million annual page-views it has today. Bill realized that while so many millions of people used Excel on a daily basis, few really knew about the incredible time- and work-saving power hidden behind the familiar grid – Visual Basic for Applications (VBA).

Bill's philosophy is simple, yet powerful. He sees himself as an Excel user – not a programmer. He believes that there are two ways to program any application: an easy way and a right way. The easy way may be quick and efficient from the programmer's perspective, but the right way is intuitively obvious from the user's perspective. And that is the addictive charm that continues to bring users back to MrExcel.com for more.

The MrExcel Network of Consultants has provided Excel, Access, & Microsoft Office applications software and automation to hundreds of clients. Now providing solutions for all Microsoft Office applications and Visual Basic programming, the MrExcel Network of Consultants has provided software and automation to over 200 clients in 2002.

Bill is co-author of "MrExcel ON EXCEL" (480 pages ISBN 0-9724258-3-7) and "Holy Macro! It's 1,600 Excel VBA Examples" CD (ISBN 0-9724258-1-0).

Bill and his wife Mary Ellen live near Akron, Ohio with their sons Josh and Zeke. When he is not programming world-class applications, Bill is active in the Goodyear Lighter Than Air Society, The Drive In Theatre Fan Club, the Rotary Club of Lake Township, the Chambers of Commerce for Lake Township, Uniontown, and Akron, and the Notre Dame Alumni Club of Akron.

Acknowledgements

The author would like to acknowledge the following persons:

Linda DeLonais & Anne Troy for excellent editing of the book; Tracy Syrstad for technical editing; Jerry Kohl for prompting the entire discussion on CSE formulas vs. pivot tables; Chank Diesel for font design; Cecilia Sveda for logo design; Scott Pierson for graphic design; Ivana Taylor for the forward, marketing wisdom and book proofing; John Sancin for pushing me to develop the book; Roy Rubin, Christine Evans and Sue Grzybowski for cover design; Mary Ellen, Josh, and Zeke Jelen for putting up with me being chained to the computer when I should have been swimming; John Walkenbach for inspiration; every MrExcel.com reader who has ever sent in a question for teaching me about Excel; Kevin Adkins for being the first to say "you should write a book"; Vicky Fowler for having to put up with my early macros; Juan Pablo Gonzalez, Mala Singh, Wei Jiang, Suat Ozgur, and Duane Aubin for handling my work while I wrote the book; Mike Absher for vehicles; every valued client at MrExcel for allowing me to hone these skills; Khalil Matta and Gary Kern for designing the killer Lotus test in 1985 that started this whole thing; the MrExcel MVPs for getting me out of a jam whenever I am in one; Ivan Moala for being at the message board since day one; Shirl Matz for general business advice and encouragement; Mike Sitek for being a VP capable of learning a CSE formula; Peter Selden for the GoTo Special trick; Pam Gensel for the first lessons in Excel macros; Dan Bricklin and Bob Frankston for being the fathers of the modern spreadsheet software; Bill Gates and the entire Microsoft Excel development team for making Excel so advanced; both Bob Jelens for their positive influence; Carol Dacoros, Pat Finnan, and Tom Hagar for being a great legal and accounting team; and Jeff Bissell for concepts regarding the SUMIF chapter. I thank you all!

Guerilla Data Analysis Using Microsoft Excel

Table of contents

Foreword

You wouldn't normally designate a technical Book like this as a page-turner, but if you're someone who has to process large amounts of data and turn it into information that's critical to a management decision then trust me – it *is* a page-turner!

If you could have seen me while I read this book, you would have seen me nodding my head in agreement and muttering phrases like "How did you know?!" or "Yes, yes, yes – that's *exactly* what happens!" or "So *that's* how you do that!" Bill Jelen – where were you during the preparation for my last staff meeting??

But no more! Now I have this remarkable "Everyman's Tool" for Excel and I'm going to be a hero. In fact, I'm getting another copy because someone is bound to steal this one or it will just plain wear out from use.

Don't believe me – go ahead and read it for yourself and you'll see what I mean.

Bill Jelen uses his combined experience and analytical ingenuity to de-mystify the arduous task of dealing with downloaded data. He uses real-life examples of real-life management requests, and then walks you through the maze of Excel tools and formulas that not only cuts valuable time out of the process, but teaches you in plain English how to overcome the most common analytical obstacles.

Now you can truly unleash the power of Excel and get the world's most powerful analytical tools to work for you – instead of the other way around.

The beauty of this book is that the author is a living, breathing, 24/7 resource for all of your Microsoft Office needs at www.MrExcel.com. If your problem or question isn't in the book, chances are there's a solution just a few clicks away.

Go ahead: breathe easy and read on . . .

-Ivana S. Taylor
Third Force Marketing

Introduction

The day before this book was to go to the printer, a storm ripped through my area. Dozens of utility poles snapped and 20,000 homes were without electricity. Cursing my luck, I packed up an old laptop and headed out into the darkness, to set up a temporary office overnight in a motel and attempted to carry on business without my files and with only a 26K phone connection. It was a valuable reminder of what can go wrong when you have a deadline. It had been two years since I packed up and walked out of corporate life, a life where stupid problems regularly arise hours or minutes before the deadline. I recalled the days when the corporate network crashed during the accounting close, or when Craig – the only guy who could operate the Fiery to run our Xerox Color Copier – simply gave up and walked out two hours before the board meeting.

If you are reading this book, the chances are that you face this stuff every week. One insane deadline is met with a breath of relief, and then you jump back in to face another insane deadline. The odds are that you are too busy fighting fires to take the time to find a faster way.

Thanks for buying this book. I hope you'll learn some great tips and techniques. My wish for you is that you never again fear walking into the board meeting to hear the CEO screaming that the analysis is screwed up. May you have endless days of data that sorts correctly and VLOOKUPs that find their match.

-Bill Jelen

In the trenches

Mainframe data is never perfect. There is a long backlog for requests at the average IT Department. Because we cannot get information in a timely manner from the IT guys, the user departments have to take things into their own hands.

The MIS Department is a willing ally in this regard. Realizing that they are understaffed, they will often purchase a 4th GL reporting tool and foist that on the user community in the hope that some users can "serve themselves" and run their own reports.

Serve Yourself

Jack Vogel introduced "Serve Yourself" counters as a quick way to get 200 carloads of drive-in movie patrons through the line during a 15-minute intermission. While "Serve Yourself" is great for drive-ins, it is not the optimal way to satisfy the need for information.

The people who designed these products realized their product's shortcomings and they offered one way out. Instead of sending a report to the green-bar printer, you could download the detail to a Lotus 1-2-3 file.

I began using a product called EZIQ from Pansophic in 1989. Fourth GL was just coming to the forefront, and this product had numerous problems. It was possible to group by customer number and sum twenty fields, but if you wanted the customer name as well, the detailed version of the report was cumbersome and hard to read. You could calculate a gross profit percentage on the detail lines, but at the total line, your only choices were to sum or average the gross profit percentage from the detail lines. If you are reading this book, I don't have to tell you that neither option makes sense.

The first week of EZIQ was rough. I was a young Data Analyst, recently promoted from the MIS Department, trying to sell the concept that "Sure! You have gross profit percentage on every detail line. Why do you need the gross profit percentage for the entire division??" It didn't play well in Minnetonka.

I had been casually using Lotus 1-2-3 since 1985. I had some basic programming skills. I figured that between my knowledge of Lotus and some basic data processing concepts, I could use Lotus 1-2-3 as the engine for producing the final reports. So, after finding a way to download the Lotus *.wks file from the IBM Mainframe to Lotus, I began using the spreadsheet to actually do the bulk of the data processing.

Do you feel safe eliminating your job?

Warning: The concepts you learn in this book are very powerful. You are going to learn how to be more efficient with Excel. I guarantee that one out of eight people reading this will learn techniques that will save your company 20 to 40 man-hours per week.

My goal is for you to keep this book on your bookshelf – always within easy reach.

If the twenty to forty hours a week of saved time is time for which you are currently receiving a paycheck, then you may be reluctant to automate your way out of a job.

If you think this is your situation, then you need to get your company to adopt the following policy.

Telxon grew from a $100 million to $500 million company while I was there. The founders made one thing very clear: If you were smart enough to find a way to eliminate your own job, you would not be rewarded with a pink slip. The company policy was to give you someone else's job. We rewarded people who could find efficiencies and punished those who kept doing things the old way.

This is such a common-sense approach to business; your CEO will be bound to adopt it.

If this isn't an explicit policy at your company, photocopy this sidebar and pass it on to your CEO anonymously.

From 1989 to 1998, some portion of my job involved taking mainframe data to Lotus, and later to Excel, and using the spreadsheet to sort, summarize, format, and print reports.

During the Fourth-GL Reporting Package sales presentation, the VPs of Finance were given a demo that made it appear that they were buying a tool that could generate a custom green-bar report in about 10 minutes. No one was smart enough during that presentation to ask if you could calculate a gross profit percentage on the total line, so we were stuck. The point is that the managers expected SPEED.

There were advantages to the fourth GL Tool, however. Early on, ninety percent of the reports that I created were ad-hoc. "We have a problem with product line A," they might have said. "Tell us everyone who has that product." These are requests that would have taken a day for a COBOL programmer, and I could have the data in a spreadsheet in about an hour.

The Fourth GL tool, even with its warts and shortcomings, did offer a faster way to get the ad-hoc data out of the mainframe and to the desks of the decision makers.

The volume of requests increased, and when we hit upon a useful report, it would be added to the list for monthly distribution.

During those first few years, I only had the ability to query history, and only at the end of the month. This kept the volume of requests to a low roar and allowed me to perfect the techniques that I teach you in this book.

I'll also walk you through several case scenarios and how we dealt with them. I'll walk you through the detailed steps of how to deal with and solve these problems in Microsoft Excel.

My goal is to explain the concept in plain English – no "programmer-speak." This book is aimed at accountants, marketers, financial or operations analysts, administrative assistants – anyone who has a large volume of data and needs to get that data into a meaningful format. You might think that I would start with that super-power of Excel data analysis – the pivot table – but I'm going to start with far more pedestrian tasks. Read through these, learn what methods are there, and then, weeks from now, you can refer to this book when you run into a similar problem.

Changing formulas to values

In case you don't already know how to convert a range to values, here is an example.

A concatenation formula joins two or more fields together.

A #REF! Error indicates that one of the cells Excel needs to calculate a formula is missing.

Excel is fantastic at performing calculations. Sometimes, we need to have Excel temporarily calculate something and we need to change the formulas to values. I refer to this technique dozens of times in this book.

One day I received a call from one of the marketing staffers in the company. She had purchased a list of data, and this data included the telephone number and the area code in separate columns as shown below.

	A	B	C
1	Name	Area Code	Telephone
2	Mary Chicago	312	555-1212
3	John Smith	401	555-1234
4	Fred Flintsone	512	555-2332
5	Bob Jelen	643	555-0000
6	Harry Houdini	718	555-9999

She wanted to combine the area code and telephone number into a single field. I showed her how to use a concatenation formula to create the desired results.

	A	B	C	D	E
1	Name	Area Code	Telephone		
2	Mary Chicago	312	555-1212	="("&B2&") "&C2	
3	John Smith	401	555-1234	(401) 555-1234	
4	Fred Flintsone	512	555-2332	(512) 555-2332	
5	Bob Jelen	643	555-0000	(643) 555-0000	
6	Harry Houdini	718	555-9999	(718) 555-9999	

She was thrilled. Before she knew of this formula, she believed she was going to have to manually retype over 1,000 telephone numbers.

Commonly, Excel novices would now either hide or delete columns B and C. Deleting these columns will have disastrous results. The formatted telephone numbers that were in column D will change to #REF! errors. The #REF! error is Excel's way of saying that you have a formula, and that you have deleted one of the cells needed to calculate that formula.

	A	B
1	Name	
2	Mary Chicago	#REF!
3	John Smith	#REF!
4	Fred Flintsone	#REF!
5	Bob Jelen	#REF!
6	Harry Houdini	#REF!

When this occurs, immediately hit **Ctrl+Z** to undo the deletion of the columns. The #REF! errors go away.

Spreadsheet veterans may remember this as the /Range Value feature of Lotus. It is just as simple in Excel.

Before you can safely delete the B and C columns, you need to change the formulas in column D to values.

Step	Procedure	Description
❑ Step 1	Highlight the range of formulas.	
❑ Step 2	Hit Ctrl+C.	*This copies the range.*
❑ Step 3	Without changing the selection, select Edit→Paste Special.	*The Paste Special dialog box displays.*
❑ Step 4	Click Values in the Paste section, then click OK.	*Your formula changes to values.*

The shortcut for Paste Special Values is <Alt>esv<Enter>.

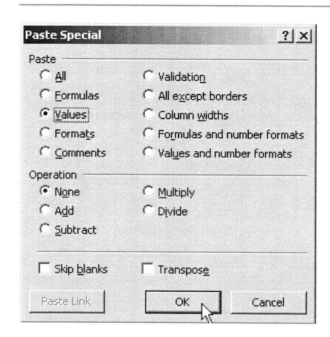

Throughout this book, I advise you to "Paste Special Values" into some range or another. When you see those instructions, I am referring to this technique.

I find that I do Paste Special Values a lot. My fingers can perform the shortcut keys: <Alt>esv<Enter> while I'm sleeping!

Other uses for Paste Special

Performing a calculation on every cell in a range

This technique can also be used to multiply a range by a certain number, or subtract, or divide.

This is somewhat obscure, but if you wanted to add the number 2 to every cell in a range of 10,000 cells, it is simple to do so without a formula.

Step	Procedure	Description
❑ Step 1	Enter the number 2 in an empty cell.	
❑ Step 2	Copy that cell.	*Select the cell and enter Ctl+C.*
❑ Step 3	Select your 10,000-row range.	

Step	Procedure	Description
❑ Step 4	Choose Edit→ Paste Special→ Add→OK.	*This adds the number 2 to every cell.*

Changing text that looks like numbers to real numbers

Some data sources provide numbers that Excel sees as text. Text that looks like numbers is great when you need to keep the leading zeroes (for example, U.S. Zip codes), but lousy when you want to perform calculations on the numbers. Excel 2002's smart tags let you correct this automatically, but for Excel 2000 and before, use the "Multiply-by-One Technique":

Step	Procedure	Description
❑ Step 1	Enter the number 1 in a blank cell.	
❑ Step 2	Copy that cell.	*Select the cell and enter* Ctl+C.
❑ Step 3	Highlight the range of text that looks like numbers and choose Edit→Paste Special→ Multiply→OK.	*The text changes to numbers.*

Transposing a column to a row

If you have headings running down a column and you want to have them run across the rows, the Paste Special command is the answer.

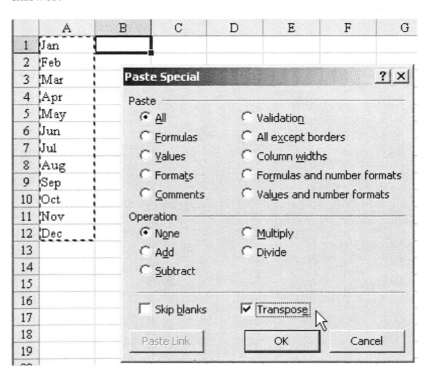

To transpose columns to rows, follow this procedure:

Step	Procedure	Description
❏ Step 1	Highlight the original range of data and copy it.	*Select the range and enter* Ctl+C.
❏ Step 2	Move the cellpointer to a new location.	*Select the cell where you want the new heading to start.*
❏ Step 3	Select Edit→Paste Special→ Transpose→OK.	*See the illustration below.*

The Transpose process takes text from a column and transposes it to a row so that it can be used as a heading.

	A	B	C	D	E	F	G	H	I	J	K	L	M
1	Jan	Jan	Feb	Mar	Apr	May	Jun	Jul	Aug	Sep	Oct	Nov	Dec
2	Feb												
3	Mar												
4	Apr												
5	May												
6	Jun												
7	Jul												
8	Aug												
9	Sep												
10	Oct												
11	Nov												
12	Dec												
13													
14													

Preserving borders

Use the "All except borders" option to avoid changing the borders.

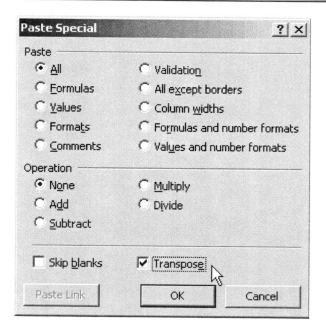

Look at the Paste Special dialog shown above. There are a lot of cool uses for Paste Special. I often find that if I have borders set up around a range and attempt to copy a formula, the borders routinely misbehave. Using the "All except borders" option is a great way to avoid changing the borders.

Multiple customer names/single customer number

The saga of XYZ

Let's say that your company has a Customer number to uniquely identify each customer. Now let's follow the life of the XYZ Company, customer number 12345.

Suppose that this company places monthly orders with you and has been doing so for the past five years. There have been two particular events in the history of your relationship with this company.

The first event was fairly significant: XYZ Company was originally the ABC Company until three years ago when they merged with XYZ Company. All orders for the first two years of your data show the account number as 12345, and the company as ABC Plastics, Inc. Then, three years ago, their data began appearing as XYZ Company with the account number 12345.

The second event, far less significant, was just as troubling: Your company hired a new Accounts Payable clerk. This A/P clerk was super-efficient and a little obsessive/compulsive. Who knows why, but one Friday afternoon, the A/P clerk decided to take the top ten accounts and do some customer maintenance. The customer names had abbreviations based on whoever set them up. The A/P clerk edited these names for consistency. Recent orders show XYZ as "YXZ Corporation, Boise ID".

The problem of dealing with multiple customer names for a single customer number is sure to strike you if the source of your data is an Invoice Register or Order Entry System.

The saga of XYZ explains how the XYZ Company became the XYZ Corporation, Boise, Idaho. The names look neater, huh? But now, every time you query the invoice register, you could have up to three names associated with the account number 12345. Here is a sample of the data:

	A	B
1	**Account #**	**Company Name**
2	12345	ABC Plastics, Inc.
3	12345	ABC Plastics, Inc.
4	12345	XYZ Company
5	12345	XYZ Company
6	12345	XYZ Company
7	12345	XYZ Corporation, Boise ID
8	12345	XYZ Corporation, Boise ID

The problem with this data is that you really want your reports to show the same customer name for all of these records.

VLOOKUP

The solution? The VLOOKUP function allows us to solve this problem. Here is the syntax for the VLOOKUP function:

=VLOOKUP(Cell to lookup, Range w/Values, Column to Return, False)

The traditional use of VLOOKUP is illustrated by this example: 10,000 rows of mainframe sales data may include a field on each record with a Sales Rep Number. This is wonderful for anyone who can memorize all 95 Sales Rep Numbers, but not so wonderful for the division VP who would rather see "Kranicki, James J." instead of "032". It is common to have a separate Excel file that lists each Sales Rep Number and the corresponding Sales Rep Name. This small file might have 95 rows and just two columns. I would typically copy this data to an out-of-the-way location on my spreadsheet, say, I2:J96.

	A	B	C	D	E	F	G
1	Acct	Company Name	Date	Revenue	Cost	Rep #	Rep Name
2	12345	ABC Plastics, Inc.	4/1/98	22000	14300	032	
3	12345	ABC Plastics, Inc.	4/1/99	2000	1300	032	
4	12345	XYZ Company	5/1/99	15000	9750	032	
5	12345	XYZ Company	7/1/00	11000	7150	128	
6	12345	XYZ Company	9/1/00	15000	9750	128	
7	12345	XYZ Corporation, B	3/1/01	43000	27950	128	
8	12345	XYZ Corporation, B	5/1/01	39000	25350	198	

Any number of things can go wrong with a VLOOKUP, from data that isn't found, to data that isn't properly formatted. Using a False argument can help!

False argument:

The false parameter — the fourth argument in this VLOOKUP — is an evil plot intended to punish power users of Lotus 1-2-3.

Decision makers are not power users of Lotus. After the decision makers forced their companies to switch from Lotus 1-2-3 to Microsoft Excel, they had little problem using their Lotus skills in Excel — the SUM and AVERAGE formulas worked just fine. Power users, however, found their VLOOKUPs no longer worked, causing angst and consternation. This discovery always comes when you are trying to power analyze.

It wasn't until someone who had already endured the pain told me, "Just add a ',FALSE' as the fourth parameter.", that everything finally fell into place.

=VLOOKUP(F2,$I$2:$J$96,2,FALSE)

This formula tells Excel to take the Rep # from F2, then cruise through all of the values in I2:I96 looking for a match. When Excel finds the matching Rep #, it then returns the second column from the table in I:J, which in this case is the rep name in J.

F	G	H	I	J
Rep #	Rep Name		Rep #	Rep Name
032	=VLOOKUP(F2,$I$2:$J$96,2,FALSE)		001	Smith, Bob
032	Kranicki, Jim		002	Myers, Lori
032	Kranicki, Jim		004	Andy, Rich
128	Chico, Maria		032	Kranicki, Jim
128	Chico, Maria		056	Back, Jon
128	Chico, Maria		128	Chico, Maria
198	#N/A		032	Jim Kranicki

Problems can occur with the VLOOKUP function. In our example, a common problem could be that the representative cannot be found in the Representatives table. For instance, Representative 198 was just hired last week, and has not yet been added to the table where we used VLOOKUP to get the representative's name, and we end up with the dreaded #N/A error.

But what about the opposite problem? We don't have anything forcing the representatives name to be unique, so it is common that a representative might appear twice in the lookup table.

This is what happened with Representative 032: Someone thought that they were a new rep and added them to the table, so they now appear a second time. If a sales rep number is in the table twice, the VLOOKUP formula returns the name associated with the first matching Rep # in the table.

Going back to our example, this behavior works exactly to our advantage! Our goal is to replace the diverse account names in column B with just a single account name for every occurrence of the account number.

To create a VLOOKUP formula, follow this procedure:

Step	Procedure	Description
❏ Step 1	Insert a temporary column C labeled "Company II".	
❏ Step 2	In column C, insert this formula: =VLOOKUP(A2,$A$2: $B$10000,2,FALSE).	
❏ Step 3	Copy the formula down to all cells using the fill handle.	*The resulting formula returns the exact results that we need.*

To use the Fill Handle:

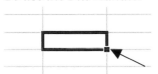

Click and drag down to copy a formula; double-click to auto-copy down many cells, as long as there is data in the adjacent column(s).

If you have a slow PC, you may find that the VLOOKUP formula can take a long time. As soon as this calculation is complete, I like to change those formulas to values. This is always a good idea; but because of the long recalculation times of VLOOKUP, it is an especially good idea.

	A	B	C
1	Acct	Company Name	Company II
2	12345	ABC Plastics, Inc.	=VLOOKUP(A2,$A$2:$B$10000,2,FALSE)
3	12345	ABC Plastics, Inc.	ABC Plastics, Inc.
4	12345	XYZ Company	ABC Plastics, Inc.
5	12345	XYZ Company	ABC Plastics, Inc.
6	12345	XYZ Company	ABC Plastics, Inc.
7	12345	XYZ Corporation, B	ABC Plastics, Inc.
8	12345	XYZ Corporation, B	ABC Plastics, Inc.

To convert formulas to values in any workbook, follow this procedure:

Benefits of changing formulas to values:

➢ Avoids #REF! Errors

➢ Reduces the recalculation time

Step	Procedure	Description
❏ Step 1	Select the range with the formulas.	*Highlight the target range.*
❏ Step 2	From the Edit menu, choose Edit→Copy.	
❏ Step 3	From the Edit menu, choose Edit→Paste Special→ Values→OK.	*You now have a single customer name for each account number.*

However, this solution is not the best one. The name, "ABC Plastics" is from an old transaction. It would be better to have the customer name from the most recent transaction shown.

Solution 1a: To sort or not to sort.

If the data can be sorted and you have a transaction date, you can use this trick:

> **Use this procedure if you can sort your data by another column.**

Step	Procedure
❑ Step 1	Sort all data by descending transaction date.
❑ Step 2	Create your VLOOKUP formula as shown above.
❑ Step 3	Convert the formulas to values.
❑ Step 4	Sort all of the data by the original sort criteria.

If you are unable to sort the data by some other column, try this:

> **Use this procedure if you cannot sort your data by some other column.**

Step	Procedure
❑ Step 1	Add a temporary column called "Sequence".
❑ Step 2	Add a sequence number, i.e., 1, 2, 3 using one of the following methods: ➢ Type 1, 2, 3 into the first three cells. Select the cells and copy down using the Fill Handle. ➢ Type 1 in the first cell. Using A2 as the cell that the 1 is typed into, type =A2+1 in cell A3. Copy the formula down using the Fill Handle. Convert these formulas to values.
❑ Step 3	Create your VLOOKUP formula.
❑ Step 4	Convert the formulas to values.
❑ Step 5	Sort your data back by sorting the Sequence column.
❑ Step 6	Delete the Sequence column.

VLOOKUP left

VLOOKUPs are great when the information you are looking for is to the right of the key field. What happens when the field you want is to the left of your key field? In the example below, we need a way to find the revenue from column C associated with an order number in column D.

It would be cool if the third parameter of VLOOKUP could be a negative number to indicate that you want a column to the LEFT of the key, but it doesn't work this way.

	A	B	C	D	E	F
1	CUST #	CUSTOMER	REVENUE	ORDER #	DATE	
2	75633	UAT GMBH	1800	12345	8/11/2002	
3	13439	CCU CORP.	2100	12346	8/11/2002	
4	19716	SZG LTD.	2400	12347	8/11/2002	
5	86993	QGH GMBH	2700	12348	8/11/2002	
6	16536	YJN GMBH	1850	12349	8/12/2002	
7	84981	SBK CO.	4100	12350	8/12/2002	
8						
9		Order				
10		12349	=VLOOKUP(B10,$C$2:$D$7,-1,FALSE)			
11						

The quick and dirty way is to copy the revenue to a temporary column F, do the VLOOKUP, convert the range formulas to values, then delete the temporary column F.

There is a better way! Unfortunately, it involves two seldom-used functions. I always find that I can learn to use one new function, but trying to master two functions at once is tough. Hang with me, though, as I walk through these in English:

=INDEX(A2:C99,3,2)

The above formula returns the third row and the second column from the range A2:C99. This is one of those functions that seems really useless, right? But let's see if we can use this in our customer example. We need a way to specify a Row # on the fly:

=INDEX(C2:C7,OurRow#,1)

Combine MATCH with INDEX to do a lookup to the left of your key field.

There is a MATCH function, which is similar to VLOOKUP. The MATCH function finds a matching value in a range of values. Instead of returning the results from another column like VLOOKUP, the MATCH function returns the relative row # of the match within the range – exactly what we need as the 2nd parameter in the INDEX function..

=MATCH(12349,D2:D99,FALSE)

This formula returns 5 because 12349 is found in cell D6, which is the fourth row of D2:D99.

The MATCH function is a great way to identify the OurRow# parameter for the INDEX function above. If you combine these two functions, you get this formula:

=INDEX(C2:C7,MATCH(B1,D2:D7,FALSE),1)

	A	B	C	D	E	F	
1	CUST #	CUSTOMER	REVENUE	ORDER #	DATE		
2	75633	UAT GMBH	1800	12345	8/11/2002		
3	13439	CCU CORP.	2100	12346	8/11/2002		
4	19716	SZG LTD.	2400	12347	8/11/2002		
5	86993	QGH GMBH	2700	12348	8/11/2002		
6	16536	YJN GMBH	1850	12349	8/12/2002		
7	84981	SBK CO.	4100	12350	8/12/2002		
8							
9		Order					
10		12349	=INDEX(C2:C7,MATCH(B10,D2:D7,FALSE),1)				
11							
12							

In English, this formula tells Excel to search through the order numbers in D2:D7 looking for a match to the order number found in cell B10. When a match is found, Excel goes to the same relative row number of C2:C7 to return the result.

So, the answer is:

=INDEX(A2:A99,MATCH(12345,D2:D99,FALSE),1)

Avoiding #NA in VLOOKUP

#N/As are difficult to work with in Excel. Anything plus #N/A is #N/A. If any term in a calculation is #N/A, then the answer is #N/A

Combine MATCH with ISNA to return zero instead of #NA.

When VLOOKUP doesn't find a match, the answer is #N/A.

Let's say we have a list of sales reps and a second list of orders by sales reps. The second list only has totals for the sales reps who actually sold something this month.

If we use a traditional VLOOKUP to populate the sales, then the information for the two reps without any sales appears as #N/A, and that district's total returns #N/A.

In this case, when the rep is not found, we want the formula to return zero instead of #N/A.

There is a function called ISNA() that allows us to detect a #N/A value and deal with it appropriately. The function returns true if the expression results in a #N/A.

One method is to actually put the VLOOKUP twice in the formula, as shown:

=IF(ISNA(VLOOKUP(A2,REPORDERS!A2:B99,2,FALSE)),0, VLOOKUP(A2,REPORDERS!A2:B99,2,FALSE))

This formula returns zero instead of #N/A. However, since VLOOKUP is not the fastest function, you almost hate to use it twice in a single formula.

Again, we can use the MATCH function instead of the first VLOOKUP in the ISNA() function as shown:

=IF(ISNA(MATCH(A2,REPS!A2:B99,FALSE)),0,VLOOKUP (A2,REPS!A2:B99,2,FALSE))

Remember, this is important because *any* #N/A in a range that is summed causes the total to report #N/A.

Using ISNA() causes missing sales figures to appear as 0, allowing the totals to work.

	A	B	C	D
1	Boston District Sales			
2	002	Myers, Lori	125,000	
3	004	Andy, Rich	0	
4	056	Back, Jon	0	
5	128	Chico, Maria	250,000	
6	**District Total**		375,000	
7	C2 is =IF(ISNA(MATCH(A2,$E$2:$E$153,FALSE)),0,VLOOKUP(A2,$E$2:$F$153,2,FALSE))			

All sorts of sorts

Toolbar trick: If you hold the shift key down while clicking on the ![A↓] *or* ![Z↓] *toolbar button, the opposite result occurs. If you're hurting for space on your toolbar, you can drag buttons off by holding the* Alt *key down and dragging the button into the spreadsheet area.*

Sorting data is a common task, so let's cover the shortcuts so you can sort in a few mouse clicks instead of many mouse clicks.

The key to sorting fast is by using the ![A↓] (sort ascending) or ![Z↓] (sort descending) buttons on the Standard toolbar.

Before using the sorting toolbar buttons, you must make deadly sure that your data is set up correctly.

Here are the rules for putting your data into a standard list format. Why are these rules important? When using either of the sorting toolbar buttons, Excel "guesses" at two things: The shape of the range you are sorting, and the answer to the "with headings or without headings" option button in the standard sort dialog box. View the sort dialog by choosing Data→Sort from the menu.

Sorting rules

Rule 1: Columns must have headings

All columns in your data must have headings. Only Microsoft knows the exact logic they use to guess headings. I've found that if any cell in row 1 of your sort range is blank, then Excel assumes your data does not contain headings and sorts the headings down into the data as though they, too, were data, which is usually an undesired result.

There are many times in this book where I advocate inserting a temporary column into your data. These are the kinds of columns that tend not to contain headings and can cause Excel to misguess the "headings" question.

Microsoft advocates changing the formatting of your heading row to bold to help Excel make this guess. This generally is not necessary, because your headings are text and some of your data is numeric, so there is a significant enough difference between your headings and your data that Excel guesses correctly. If your headings contain numeric entries, applying a swath of bold formatting can help.

Rule 2: Headings must be only one cell tall

Each heading must consist of exactly one cell. Excel is only smart enough to deal with one row of headings. There is no option to have Excel's sort buttons work with multiple heading rows that need to be untouched during sort.

So, what if you have a long heading that needs two lines as shown on the following page?

	A	B	C	D	E	F	G
1			Unit	Unit		Gross	
2	Order	Quantity	Price	Cost	Revenue	Profit	GP%
3							
4							

Use Alt+Enter *to place a line break within a cell.*

The answer is to enter a two-line heading into a single cell. Instead of typing Unit in C1 and Price in C2, click on cell C1 and type Unit. Then hit Alt+Enter and type Price. The Alt+Enter key combination places a line break within the cell. The following graphic depicts the use of this layout; cells have been vertically aligned to the bottom of the cell.

Excel can sort correctly when your headings are in this single-row format.

	A	B	C	D	E	F	G
1	Order	Quantity	Unit Price	Unit Cost	Revenue	Gross Profit	GP%
2							
3							

Rule 3: No completely blank rows or columns

There should be no completely blank rows or completely blank columns in your data. Excel has to guess which range you are trying to sort and does an amazing job if you follow this rule.

Excel calls this range the "Current Region". When you click on a cell and hit one of the AZ sorting buttons, Excel sorts the current region around that cell.

The simplest, but least intuitive way to explain Current Region is that Excel extends the range in all directions until it hits the edge of the spreadsheet, or until it hits a totally blank row and/or column around the selected cell. To determine the Current Region, select a cell, hit the F5 key, choose Special, Current Region, and then examine the region that is selected.

Here are some examples of Current Regions:

Excel has no problem ignoring blank cells because there are no completely blank rows or columns.

	A	B	C	D
1	Salutation	First Name	Middle Name	Last Name
2	Mr.	Mickey	M.	Mouse
3		Donald		Duck
4	Ms.	Minnie		Mouse
5	Mr.			Excel
6	Mr.	William		Jelen

Column E is left blank when someone fills in the employee bonuses for a quickie report to the boss. When they sort their data by last name, the bonus amounts are not sorted with it.

	A	B	C	D	E	F
1	Emp Number	First Name	Middle Name	Last Name		Bonus Paid
2	12345	Mickey	M.	Mouse		$3,000.00
3	32345	Donald		Duck		$3,100.00
4	32333	Minnie		Mouse		$3,300.00
5	42344	Mister		Excel		$ 500.00
6	1234	William		Jelen		$ 400.00

This example is similar to the previous one, but the user has placed a single value in column D. This causes Excel to extend the Current Region correctly.

	A	B	C	D	E	F
1	Emp Number	First Name	Middle Name	Last Name		Bonus Paid
2	12345	Mickey	M.	Mouse		$3,000.00
3	32345	Donald		Duck	v	$3,100.00
4	32333	Minnie		Mouse		$3,300.00
5	42344	Mister		Excel		$ 500.00
6	1234	William		Jelen		$ 400.00

This example has unrelated data in the same worksheet. There is a completely blank column that breaks the Current Region. If you place any data in column E, Excel sorts your years incorrectly along with a sort of, for instance, the employee numbers, which is undesired.

	A	B	C	D	E	F	G
1	Emp Number	First Name	Middle Name	Last Name		Year	Forecasted Revenue
2	12345	Mickey	M.	Mouse		2003	20,000,000.00
3	32345	Donald		Duck		2004	23,000,000.00
4	32333	Minnie		Mouse		2005	24,000,000.00
5	42344	Mister		Excel		2005	26,000,000.00
6	1234	William		Jelen		2007	30,000,000.00

When you have areas of unrelated data in a worksheet, ensure that your data is sorted properly by having at least one completely blank row and column at the border of each area of data.

Rule 4: No named ranges called "Database"

Even if you go to the extra step of selecting the entire named database range plus the extra columns, Excel still overrides your selection and sorts only the named database range.

There should never be a named range of "Database" in your workbook. This may sound obscure, but it causes havoc. Let's suppose that instead of getting your data from a mainframe, the data came from a tool that generates dBaseIII files (*.dbf).

When importing from certain database file types, Excel adds a named range called "Database" to describe the data it added. There is certainly a good reason for this, something other than a desire to cause havoc on Microsoft's part. This range name is supposed to help with "round-tripping", the process of opening a .DBF file in Excel and then saving it back as a .DBF file.

This procedure also changes the guessing behavior of how Excel tries to figure out which range to sort. If your starting cell is in the midst of a range named "Database", the contiguous range rules are ignored if any columns you added to the side of your data are not sorted correctly.

It is fairly common to add a new column to a DBF-sourced dataset. Many properly formatted databases store less data and calculate many fields on the fly. As you are adding those calculations to Excel in order to produce a quick report for the managers' meeting, having Excel incorrectly guess the sort range can be disastrous. Always remove the named range "Database" as explained on the following page.

Here, I provide workarounds:

> If you will not be refreshing your data from the external database, delete the range name by using Insert→Name→Define.
> Select the name "Database" and hit Delete.

> Add any new columns in the middle of the range so that they will be included in the sort range.

Comparing sort techniques

With the full Sort technique, you select one cell in your sort range, click Data→Sort, and then choose to sort by District, Representative (ascending), and Revenue (descending). This is a total of ten mouse clicks.

Using the AZ sort buttons, you would click in Revenue and hit ZA↓, click in Representative and hit AZ↓, and then click in Region and hit AZ↓. This is a total of six mouse clicks.

When you need to sort by four or more columns using the full Sort dialog, you must first sort by your fourth, fifth, and sixth columns, and then sort again by your first, second, and third columns. This requires twenty mouse clicks versus the twelve required by the AZ sort buttons.

> What if your data can't be put into a list format? I once had a manager who required a one-column wide blank column to the left of six columns of data. He insisted on this so that there would be a small break between the underscores under the heading for each column.

	A	B	C	D	E	F	G	H	I	J	K	L	M
							Gross		Operating				
1	Division		Revenue		COGS		Margin		Expenses		Net Profit		NP%
2	United States		147,000		85,260		61,740		46,599		15,141		10.3%
3	Canada		13,500		6,885		6,615		5,009		1,607		11.9%
4	United Kingdom		27,501		14,300		13,201		10,065		3,136		11.4%
5	France		5,602		3,193		2,409		1,837		572		10.2%
6	Germany		3,456		1,935		1,521		1,089		432		12.5%
7	Italy		6,542		3,598		2,944		2,211		733		11.2%
8	Spain		0		0		0		814		-814		n.m.
9	Australia		5,789		3,241		2,548		1,910		638		11.0%
10	Japan		1,201		636		565		459		106		8.8%
11													
12	**TOTAL**		210,591		119,048		91,543		69,993		21,550		10.2%

Whenever I have had to work with worksheets with the blank columns used as spacers, putting them in list format and putting them back has been more trouble than it was worth. There are three workarounds in such cases:

1. You can explicitly select the entire range (A1:M10 in the above example) before using the Data→Sort dialog box.

2. You can embed a hidden heading in cells B1, D1, F1, H1, J1, and L1. I like to make this a single period in a white font.

3. You could ignore Rule 4 above and name the range A1:M10 "Database". That would cause Excel to sort the entire range, blank columns and all.

Matching two lists of data

I used to manage the forecasting process for a medium-sized company. The sales representatives were supposed to maintain a monthly forecast by customer. Every day, I could download the most up-to-date forecasts by customer from the sales force. Also daily, I could download a summary of open orders and billed invoices for the month by customer. The challenge was then to match up the two lists to produce a summary of what orders had come in and which orders were still expected to come in.

There were several challenges in matching these items.

> First, the sales representatives would never bother to forecast the small orders. When an order came in for some spare batteries, you could bet that there would be an order in the order list without a matching forecast in the first list.

> Second, the sales reps were always optimistic. There were several items on the forecast list that would never materialize each month.

> Third, sales reps are notorious for rounding up when they produce their forecast. An order for $98,000 would usually be forecasted as $100,000. This is to be expected. However, our sales reps were especially talented at rounding up. Pretty much anything above $80,000 was rounded up to $100,000.

> Fourth, none of our sales reps enjoyed forecasting. It was seen as a burden. It was actually an amazing thing when a sales rep said he was going to sell $100K to XYZ and an order came in from XYZ for about $95K.

> For various reasons, our customer master database always seemed to have four customer numbers for XYZ. There was the number for the West Coast division, the East Coast Division, the corporate headquarters, then one setup because the person searching for the account typed in "X Y Z", didn't see the account and set up a new account.

As a data analyst, I was familiar with account numbers and would have paid attention to the account numbers and put the right account number on the forecast. Of course, our sales representatives were lucky to get any account number for XYZ on the forecast.

The process of matching these two lists actually involves doing two matches. These two steps will apply to almost any situation where you need to match two lists.

> First, you have to find accounts that are on the forecast but not yet on order.

> Second, these "new" accounts need to be added to the orders report so that the orders contains a complete superset of all the accounts on either the forecast or the order report.

The forecast data called for sales of $21.5 million this month. It is comprised of three columns — an account number, the customer name, and the forecasted revenue for the month.

	A	B	C
1	**Cust#**	**Customer Name**	**Forecast**
2	13914	PXY LTD.	425,000
3	14884	NFP GMBH	475,000
4	15934	QEL, INC.	375,000
5	19716	BLS S.A.	65,000
6	27542	UKU GMBH	700,000
7	29889	TOL, INC.	542,000
8	34399	NPC CORP.	200,000
9	36633	HZT LTD.	3,000,000
10	36694	BJK S.A.	125,000
11	37935	WCO S.A.	2,500,000
12	43226	HAD S.A.	2,500,000

The orders data shows open or billed orders of $20.5 million for this month. This data also has an account number, a customer number, then columns for amount invoiced, open orders and a total.

	A	B	C	D	E
1	**Cust#**	**Customer Name**	**Invoiced**	**Open Orders**	**Total**
2	11321	LIB S.A.	9,000	0	9,000
3	11831	KYZ LTD.	0	5,200	5,200
4	13914	PXY LTD.	405,000	0	405,000
5	14884	NFP GMBH	61,000	244,000	305,000
6	19716	BLS S.A.	0	55,000	55,000
7	22615	KBI LTD.	747,000	498,000	1,245,000
8	27542	UKU GMBH	0	750,000	750,000
9	34399	NPC CORP.	0	205,000	205,000
10	36633	HZT LTD.	0	2,005,000	2,005,000
11	37935	WCO S.A.	0	2,151,200	2,151,200
12	43226	HAD S.A.	3,005,000	0	3,005,000
13	44736	OOU, INC.	0	10,000	10,000
14	45253	ARZ, INC.	33,000	22,000	55,000
15	45523	BGY GMBH	0	210,000	210,000
16	54185	VBB LTD.	5,500	0	5,500
17	55443	AUM CORP.	0	2,456,000	2,456,000
18	56581	OTP LTD.	0	35,000	35,000
19	57165	XHJ, INC.	1,604,000	401,000	2,005,000
20	59475	YIR GMBH	0	8,000	8,000
21	65296	YBH LTD.	10,000	0	10,000
22	67981	EBG GMBH	0	305,000	305,000
23	76812	IKN GMBH	2,000,000	3,000,000	5,000,000
24	79517	STE GMBH	82,000	123,000	205,000
25	88699	PGN GMBH	0	5,500	5,500
26	96641	UOL GMBH	5,200	0	5,200
27	98194	LXH GMBH	36,000	9,000	45,000
28					20,500,600
29					

◄◄ ◄ ► ►◄ \ **Orders** / Forecast /

The MATCH formula is similar to a VLOOKUP, except it does not return any data from the lookup list.

Used by itself, the MATCH formula either returns a number that indicates which cell in A2:A27 contains the first match or, if there is no match, it returns the value #N/A.

Like VLOOKUP, MATCH only returns a single match no matter how many it finds.

The ISNA() function returns a TRUE if the value inside the function is #N/A.

To fill several cells with the same value or formula,

1. *Select all of the cells.*
2. *Type the value.*
3. *Hit* Ctrl+Enter.

The first step is to find accounts on the Forecast list that are not on the Orders list.

Step	Procedure	Description
❏ Step 1	Add a temporary "Add?" field to column D on the Forecast worksheet.	*We'll use the ISNA and MATCH functions from the VLOOKUP section in this formula, entered into cell D2 on the Forecast:.*
❏ Step 2	Enter this formula into cell D2 on the Forecast. =ISNA(MATCH(A2,Orders!$A$2:$A$27,FALSE))	*We ask Excel to take the value from A2 and to look through A2:A27 on the Orders sheet.* *The FALSE parameter, as in the VLOOKUP function, indicates that we need an exact match. Here, we are interested in the forecasts that don't have a matching record in the order database. This formula returns a TRUE whenever there is a forecast that has no matching orders.*
❏ Step 3	Copy the formula from D2 to D3:D25 on the forecast worksheet.	*You can double click the fill handle in D2 to quickly copy the formula to D3:D25.*
❏ Step 4	Insert a blank row between the total row and the detail rows.	*This ensures that the total does not get sorted into the data.*
❏ Step 5	Select cell D2 and hit the ZA↓ button to sort the TRUEs to the top of the list.	*Any record with a TRUE in column D needs to be added to the Orders worksheet.*
❏ Step 6	Copy the Customer number and name fields from the Forecast worksheet and paste these records to the end of the Orders list.	*Only copy the records where the Add? Field is True.*
❏ Step 7	Fill in zeroes for the Invoiced, Open Orders, and Total columns for these new records.	*The orders worksheet now contains a superset of all customers with orders or forecasts.*

	A	B	C	D
1	Cust#	Customer Name	Forecast	Add?
2	15934	QEL, INC.	375,000	TRUE
3	29889	TOL, INC.	542,000	TRUE
4	36694	BJK S.A.	125,000	TRUE
5	43655	PJN CO.	250,000	TRUE
6	55444	AUM CO.	2,500,000	TRUE
7	67121	OYT S.A.	185,000	TRUE
8	73957	ZHB GMBH	250,000	TRUE
9	95381	BWE CORP.	325,000	TRUE
10	13914	PXY LTD.	425,000	FALSE
11	14884	NFP GMBH	475,000	FALSE

Step	Procedure	Description
❑ Step 8	On the Orders worksheet, add a column for Forecast.	*Type the heading "Forecast" into cell F1.*
❑ Step 9	Enter this formula into cell F2 on the Orders. =VLOOKUP(A2,Forecast!$A$2:$C$25,3,FALSE)	*A quick VLOOKUP formula in column F returns the forecasted amount for each customer.*
❑ Step 10	Copy the formula from F2 to F3:F29 on the forecast worksheet.	*However, when there are unforecasted orders, the VLOOKUP formula returns the non-useful #N/A error.*

To fill several cells with the same value,

1. *Select all of the cells.*
2. *Hit* Ctrl+Enter.

	A	B	C	D	E	F
1	Cust#	Customer Name	Invoiced	Open Orders	Total	Forecast
2	11321	LIB S.A.	9,000	0	9,000	#N/A
3	11831	KYZ LTD.	0	5,200	5,200	#N/A
4	13914	PXY LTD.	405,000	0	405,000	425,000
5	14884	NFP GMBH	61,000	244,000	305,000	475,000
6	15934	QEL, INC.	0	0	0	375,000
7	19716	BLS S.A.	0	55,000	55,000	65,000
8	22615	KBI LTD.	747,000	498,000	1,245,000	#N/A
9	27542	UKU GMBH	0	750,000	750,000	700,000

Step	Procedure	Description
❑ Step 11	Enter this formula into cell F2 on the Orders. =IF(ISNA(VLOOKUP(A2, Forecast!$A$2:$C$25,3, FALSE)),0,VLOOKUP(A2, Forecast!$A$2:$C$25,3, FALSE))	*To replace the #N/A errors with 0's, we need to use the ISNA function again, this time coupled with an IF function.*

The formula in Step 11 actually does the VLOOKUP twice. First it evaluates the VLOOKUP inside of the ISNA() function to see if there is a matching forecast or not. If there is not a matching forecast, then ISNA() returns a TRUE.

In that case, the second parameter of our IF statement indicates to return a zero. Otherwise, if the ISNA() returns a FALSE, then the third parameter of our IF statement tells Excel to return the results of the VLOOKUP.

With a pair of VLOOKUPs – first a VLOOKUP from the forecast list into the order list in order to identify new forecasts, and then a second VLOOKUP from the order list to the forecast list – we've managed to overcome two problems. We've handled unforecasted orders and also forecasts without any matching orders.

Building a formula for forecast balance

We want to calculate how much of the forecast is still due to come in. A formula of =F2-E2 in column G will work for some records, but will return a negative number for others.

	A	B	C	D	E	F	G
1	Cust#	Customer Name	Invoiced	Open Orders	Total	Forecast	Forecast Balance
2	36633	HZT LTD.	0	2,005,000	2,005,000	3,000,000	995,000
3	73957	ZHB GMBH	0	0	0	250,000	250,000
4	59475	YIR GMBH	0	8,000	8,000	0	-8,000
5	27542	UKU GMBH	0	750,000	750,000	700,000	-50,000

For our first record, we had a forecast of $3 million and about $2 million is on order. In this case, the forecast balance of $995,500 is correct.

Look at the third record. In this case, an $8,000 order came in that was unforecasted. As previously noted, the sales representatives rarely forecast the smaller orders. If an order comes in that exceeds a forecast, or if an order comes in that was never forecasted, we don't want the forecasted balance to go negative.

A quick way to ensure that the results of a formula are never negative is to have a MAX function where the arguments are the original formula and a zero. Excel returns the larger number. When comparing a zero and a positive result from the formula, the result from the formula is always larger and you get the result from the original formula. When the result from the original formula is negative, the zero is larger and the MAX function returns the zero.

Use the MAX function to ensure that Excel returns a positive number when the arguments are the original number and a zero.

Change the formula in column G to be:

=MAX(0,F2-E2)

	A	B	C	D	E	F	G
1	Cust#	Customer Name	Invoiced	Open Orders	Total	Forecast	Forecast Balance
2	13914	PXY LTD.	405,000	0	405,000	425,000	20,000
3	37935	WCO S.A.	0	2,151,200	2,151,200	2,500,000	348,800
4	19716	BLS S.A.	0	55,000	55,000	65,000	10,000
5	14884	NFP GMBH	61,000	244,000	305,000	475,000	170,000
6	27542	UKU GMBH	0	750,000	750,000	700,000	0
7	59475	YIR GMBH	0	8,000	8,000	0	0

Eliminating rounding errors

As previously mentioned, sales representatives are notorious for rounding their forecasts up. In the above image, the forecast for PXY LTD. was $425,000 and orders have come in for $405,000. Since the order is within about 5% of the forecast, this seems to be a likely situation where the sales representative overstated the forecast a bit. I would like to change the forecast balance formula to zero out any forecast balances that are less than 10% of the original forecast.

This formula solves that:

=IF((F2-E2)/F2<0.1,0,MAX(F2-E2,0))

To eliminate the #DIV/0 error, surround the formula with an IF statement that checks to see if the denominator is zero.

However, when the value in E2 is 0, it returns a #DIV/0! (division by zero) error. The simple way to eliminate division by zero errors is to surround the formula in an IF statement that checks to see if the denominator is zero:

=IF(F2=0,0,IF(MAX(+F2-E2,0)/F2<0.1,0,MAX(F2-E2,0)))

Calculating total expected

In this case, the total expected for the month is the total of Invoices + Open Orders + Expected Forecast. From a logical data processing point of view, this analysis is complete. We have $20 million of orders in the system and another $6.3 million still expected from the forecast.

This type of report would be the subject of weekly sales conference calls. The VP of Sales would use this as a cheat-sheet and review all of the large "Expected Forecast" items with the sales managers. The data analysts would take notes of changes and make sure that the sales rep entered changes in the forecast system so that the next day's report would be correct.

	A	B	C	D	E	F	G	H
1	Cust#	Customer Name	Invoiced	Open Orders	Total Booked	Forecast	Forecast Balance	Total Expected
2	45253	ARZ, INC.	33,000	22,000	55,000	70,000	15,000	70,000
3	55444	AUM CO.	0	0	0	2,500,000	2,500,000	2,500,000
4	55443	AUM CORP.	0	2,456,000	2,456,000	0	0	2,456,000
5	45523	BGY GMBH	0	210,000	210,000	300,000	90,000	300,000
6	36694	BJK S.A.	0	0	0	125,000	125,000	125,000
7	19716	BLS S.A.	0	55,000	55,000	65,000	10,000	65,000
8	95381	BWE CORP.	0	0	0	325,000	325,000	325,000
9	67981	EBG GMBH	0	305,000	305,000	450,000	145,000	450,000
30	54185	VBB LTD.	5,500	0	5,500	0	0	5,500
31	37935	WCO S.A.	0	2,151,200	2,151,200	2,500,000	348,800	2,500,000
32	57165	XHJ, INC.	1,604,000	401,000	2,005,000	1,000,000	0	2,005,000
33	65296	YBH LTD.	10,000	0	10,000	0	0	10,000
34	59475	YIR GMBH	0	8,000	8,000	0	0	8,000
35	73957	ZHB GMBH	0	0	0	250,000	250,000	250,000
36								
37	Total		8,002,700	12,497,900	20,500,600	21,552,000	6,360,800	26,861,400

Manually catching errors

When you locate an error like this, it is important not only to change it on today's analysis in Excel, but also to go back to the original source data (in this case, the forecast database) and correct the error there.

This ensures that tomorrow's report won't have the same problem.

The steps involved in this chapter are no small feat and a beginning data analyst would be happy to have mastered all of those steps. (In practice, if you really had to do this daily, you would want to have a macro developed in Visual Basic for Applications that would automate all of the above steps into a single mouse click.)

I have seen many budding data analysts finish the steps needed to complete this report, only to click the print icon and immediately hand the report off to their boss. That would be a HUGE mistake!

As data analysts, we have to remember that the source of the data is based on human data entry. It is very easy for any number of errors to happen along the way. Your job is to figure out the most common errors and check for those.

Look at the data below, reproduced from the preceding page. Can you spot the obvious error?

	A	B	C	D	E	F	G	H
				Open	Total		Forecast	Total
1	Cust#	Customer Name	Invoiced	Orders	Booked	*Forecast*	Balance	Expected
2	45253	ARZ, INC.	33,000	22,000	55,000	*70,000*	15,000	70,000
3	55444	AUM CO.	0	0	0	*2,500,000*	2,500,000	2,500,000
4	55443	AUM CORP.	0	2,456,000	2,456,000	*0*	0	2,456,000
5	45523	BGY GMBH	0	210,000	210,000	*300,000*	90,000	300,000
6	36694	BJK S.A.	0	0	0	*125,000*	125,000	125,000
7	19716	BLS S.A.	0	55,000	55,000	*65,000*	10,000	65,000
8	95381	BWE CORP.	0	0	0	*325,000*	325,000	325,000
9	67981	EBG GMBH	0	305,000	305,000	*450,000*	145,000	450,000
30	54185	VBB LTD.	5,500	0	5,500	*0*	0	5,500
31	37935	WCO S.A.	0	2,151,200	2,151,200	*2,500,000*	348,800	2,500,000
32	57165	XHJ, INC.	1,604,000	401,000	2,005,000	*1,000,000*	0	2,005,000
33	65296	YBH LTD.	10,000	0	10,000	*0*	0	10,000
34	59475	YIR GMBH	0	8,000	8,000	*0*	0	8,000
35	73957	ZHB GMBH	0	0	0	*250,000*	250,000	250,000
36								
37	Total		8,002,700	12,497,900	20,500,600	*21,552,000*	6,360,800	26,861,400

As I mentioned before, it was all too common to have two or more account numbers in the system for a similar account. We were lucky to have the sales reps enter a forecast at all, let alone get the account number correct. In my experience, the sales rep would find the first customer name that looked remotely correct, and then use the corresponding customer number. In this case, the sales rep for AUM did a great job of forecasting the $2.5 million order. However, he used the wrong account number – 55444 – and the order came in under account 55443. Do you see the problem now? Look on rows 3 and 4. The forecast on row 3 calls for $2.5 million of additional expected forecast to come in. However, the order is already in – on row 4 – with a different account number. This analysis has overstated the forecast by $2.5 million.

A few seconds spent reviewing this small 34-record analysis would probably reveal the above error. In a real analysis with hundreds of records, it is much harder to immediately find such problems.

Automated error checking

With a $24 million total, it helps to manually study the 20% of the records that make up 80% of the revenue. One easy way is to sort the database by Total in column H descending. Click in H2 and slowly drag down the column to select a larger and larger range of cells. Watch the QuickSum feature in the status bar until you have selected about 80% of the revenue.

You will want to manually check those 10 to 12 records for errors.

	H	I
:ast	**Total**	
nce	**Expected**	
0	5,000,000	
0	3,005,000	
,000	3,000,000	
,800	2,500,000	
0	2,456,000	
0	2,005,000	
0	1,245,000	
0	750,000	
,000	542,000	
,000	475,000	
,000	450,000	

Sum=20,503,000

> **QuickSum feature**
>
> The QuickSum feature appears if you select two or more numeric cells. It's a great way to quickly get a total or average of a range without entering a formula. To change to average, just right-click the QuickSum in the status bar area.

We made a habit of storing today's final report to a file. Then, after completing the analysis for the next day, we would use two sets of VLOOKUPs as outlined at the beginning of this chapter to match up yesterday and today's reports. We would focus on any changes in columns E and H. This prevented us from manually having to check hundreds of records that did not change.

There is another method that you can utilize to automate the error checking process.

In the following example, column I contains the prior day's Total Booked. Column J contains the prior day's Expected Total. Columns K and L calculates the total from yesterday to today. Column M is a formula that ranks the magnitude of the change. The formula in M2 is:

=MAX(K2:L2,-MIN(K2:L2))

This ensures that large reductions and large increases are both considered a large change. Sort descending by column M and you can make sure that someone manually scans through each major change.

	A	B	E	G	H	I	J	K	L	M
1	Cust#	Customer Name	**Total Booked**	**Forecast Balance**	**Total Expected**	Prior Booked	Prior Total	Delta Booked	Delta Total	Change
2	36633	HZT LTD.	2,005,000	495,000	2,500,000	2,005K	3,000K	0K	-500K	500K
3	15934	QEL, INC.	375,000	0	375,000	0K	375K	375K	0K	375K
4	94886	KYG LTD.	0	250,000	250,000	0K	0K	0K	250K	250K
5	45523	BGY GMBH	0	300,000	300,000	210K	300K	-210K	0K	210K
6	66194	JBX S.A.	150,000	0	150,000	0K	0K	150K	150K	150K
7	29889	TOL, INC.	0	542,000	542,000	0K	542K	0K	0K	0K

In Row 3, you can verify that the forecasted amount of $375K for QEL actually came in and was entered as an order yesterday.

To display numbers in thousands, use a custom number format of #,##0,K.

Row 5 is of particular concern. There has been a $300K forecast. The Total Expected for yesterday and today remains $300K. However, as of yesterday, there had been an order booked for $210K of this amount. That order has disappeared today. Either the customer cancelled the order, or the plant re-scheduled it for another month. This is the record that warrants further examination. It is very unlikely that the forecast for this month should remain at $300K if either of those events happened. The source record in the forecast database needs to change.

Conclusion

Matching lists of data is a very common data analysis requirement. You will need to master doing two sets of VLOOKUPs – one to get a superset of all records, and then a second VLOOKUP to actually bring values from the second list to the first. Exercise great care when matching records from different sources to ensure that the results are correct.

Data→Consolidate

Often, you'll find that mainframe data has not been consolidated. It will be at the detail level instead of a summary level.

	A	B	C	D	E	F	G
1	ORDER #	DATE	CUST #	NAME	REVENUE	COST	GP
2	12345	6/27/2002	01200	ABC Co.	1800	980	46%
3	12346	6/27/2002	01862	ComCo	9288	4800	48%
4	12347	6/28/2002	01098	Achoo	4392	2800	36%
5	12348	6/28/2002	01200	ABC Co.	1800	980	46%
6	12349	6/29/2002	01862	ComCo	9288	4800	48%
7	12350	6/29/2002	01098	Achoo	4392	2800	36%

There are many ways of summarizing detailed data:

➤ Pivot tables

➤ Subtotals

➤ Consolidate

By far, consolidation is the least flexible, but there are times when it is appropriate.

Data to be consolidated needs to have the key field located on the left-most column of a named range. There should be unique headings along the top row of the data. The consolidation output totals all numeric columns and leaves the text columns blank.

Using the above data, I would like to summarize Revenue, Cost, and GP by Customer number. I prefer to use named ranges, so the first step is to assign a name like "TotMc" to C1:G999. This ensures that the data is consolidated by whatever column is in the left-most column of the range. In this case, the left-most column is column C, which contains Customer number.

Fast Range Naming:

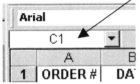

Select the range that you want to name, then type the range name into the Name box where indicated, and hit the Enter key.

Step	Procedure	Description
❏ Step 1	Select C1:G999.	
❏ Step 2	In the Name box, type **TotMe** and hit **Enter**.	
❏ Step 3	Select the cell to the upper-left of where you would like your consolidation range to appear.	*Use a blank area of the worksheet.*
❏ Step 4	Choose **Data→Consolidate** from the menu.	

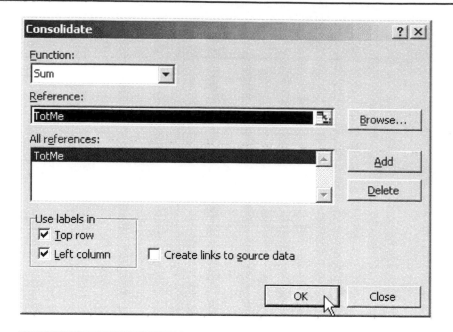

Step	Procedure	Description
☐ Step 5	In the Reference box, type TotMe.	
☐ Step 6	Place checkmarks in the Top row and Left column checkboxes and hit OK.	*The result should look similar to the following illustration.*

The Consolidate feature leaves the top left corner heading blank. You will need to fill this heading in manually.

Also, this feature works with numeric data only, not with text, so you will need to use a VLOOKUP formula to fill in any text data.

	A	B	C	D	E
1		**Name**	**Revenue**	**Cost**	**GP**
2	01200		3600	1960	91%
3	01862		18576	9600	97%
4	01098		8784	5600	72%

Note that you now have one line per customer. Strangely enough, the Consolidate feature always fails to fill in the heading in the top-left corner of the output range. It is best to fill this in manually so that you can sort your data easily.

Consolidation also works only with numeric data, so the customer name field is blank. You will have to use a VLOOKUP formula to fill in the customer names. Even with numeric data, there are times where it does not make sense to total the numeric values. This is true with dates. It is also true with the Gross Profit percentages shown in this example. You will want to enter new formulas to calculate GP% for the summary rows in the consolidation table.

Data→Subtotals and Go To Special

Automatic subtotals are a very nice feature in Excel. They were introduced in Excel 95 with one serious bug, and then corrected in Excel 97. The bug means that we will need to approach the feature two different ways when using it for multiple levels of subtotals.

Subtotaling data

Just as in my EZIQ story in the beginning of the book, Subtotals are only good at doing one calculation for every column. There is no way to calculate a gross profit percentage for the total lines using subtotals. However, once subtotaled, it is simple to add the GP% later.

Below, you see data by Region, District, and Product, with Quantity, Average Price, Revenue, and Status. Before using Subtotals, the data needs to be sorted. In the first example, we add the subtotals by product.

	A	B	C	D	E	F	G
1	Region	District	Product	Quantity	Avg Price	Revenue	Status
2	01	122	Widget	240	16.99	$4,077.60	A
3	01	122	Widget	240	16.99	$4,077.60	A
4	01	123	Premium Widget	120	24.99	$2,998.80	A
5	01	123	Premium Widget	240	17.99	$4,317.60	A
6	02	234	Quality Widget	480	17.99	$8,635.20	B
7	03	322	Deluxe Widget	480	24.99	$11,995.20	B

Step	Procedure	Description
❑ Step 1	Sort the data by Column C.	
❑ Step 2	Select any single cell in the range of data.	*This enables you to insert subtotals.*
❑ Step 3	Select **Data→Subtotals** from the menu.	

When you first create subtotals for a range, Excel makes three assumptions and prefills these into the Subtotals dialog box.

➢ Excel assumes you want to subtotal by the values in Column A.

➢ Excel assumes you want to total the last column of data.

➢ Excel looks at the last column of data and, if it is numeric, it assumes that you want to sum the values; if it is non-numeric, it assumes that you want to count the values.

In our example, all of these assumptions are wrong. So, just be aware that you need to change these defaults. The third default is particularly easy to forget.

The basic functionality of subtotals lets you add a total line at each change of a key value.

The old data processing term for this was called a Control-Break.

The default selections that you end up with after choosing Data→Subtotals will often be wrong.

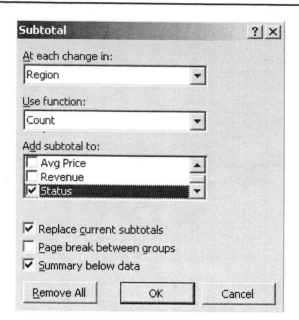

Follow these steps to correct the default selections:

Step	Procedure	Description
❏ Step 1	Select Product instead of Region in the **At each change in:** box.	*Click on the dropdown arrow to see the choices.*
❏ Step 2	Change Count to Sum in **Use function:**.	*Click on the dropdown arrow to see the choices.*
❏ Step 3	Checkmark Quantity and Revenue. Uncheck the last field – the Status field – for **Add subtotal to:**.	*You will need to scroll all the way to the bottom of the list. Excel always checkmarks the last field by default.*
❏ Step 4	Click OK.	

Subtotal dialog after changing the default selections

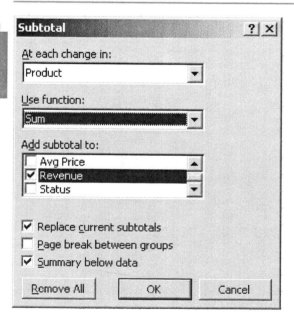

There are several things to notice about your subtotals.

> First, they have been magically inserted at each change in Product.

> Second, there are now Group and Outline buttons to the left of Row 1.

1 2 3		A	B	C	D	E	F
	1	Region	District	**Product**	**Quantity**	**Avg Price**	**Revenue**
	2	03	322	Deluxe Widget	480	24.99	$11,995.20
	3			**Deluxe Widget Total**	480		$11,995.20
	4	01	123	Premium Widget	120	24.99	$2,998.80
	5	01	123	Premium Widget	240	17.99	$4,317.60
	6			**Premium Widget Total**	360		$7,316.40

Go To Special

The Group and Outline buttons let you see:

1. just a grand total,

2. just the subtotals, or

3. the detail with subtotals.

1 2 3		A
	1	**Region**
	2	01
	3	
	4	03

The + and − buttons, like those in Windows Explorer, allow you to open and close detail views of specific groups.

When you click Outline Button 2, you see just the subtotals you need, and there is a tendency to want to copy these results to another worksheet. There is a caveat, and a workaround.

C	D	E	F
Product	**Quantity**	**Avg Price**	**Revenue**
Deluxe Widget Total	480		$11,995.20
Premium Widget Total	360		$7,316.40
Quality Widget Total	480		$8,635.20
Widget Total	480		$8,155.20
Grand Total	1800		$36,102.00

Product	Quantity	Avg Price	Revenue
Deluxe Widget	480	24.99	$11,995.20
Deluxe Widget Total	480		$11,995.20
Premium Widget	120	24.99	$2,998.80
Premium Widget	240	17.99	$4,317.60
Premium Widget Total	360		$7,316.40
Quality Widget	480	17.99	$8,635.20
Quality Widget Total	480		$8,635.20
Widget	240	16.99	$4,077.60
Widget	240	16.99	$4,077.60
Widget Total	480		$8,155.20
Grand Total	1800		$36,102.00

Caveat: When you use the "2" Group and Outline button, you see just the summary lines. However, when you copy and paste these lines to a new section of the worksheet, you actually copy the hidden rows as well.

Workaround: The solution lies in selecting "Visible cells only" in the Go To Special dialog box.

Step	Procedure	Description
❏ Step 1	Highlight your subtotals.	
❏ Step 2	From the Edit menu, select Edit→Go To.	*The Go To screen displays.*

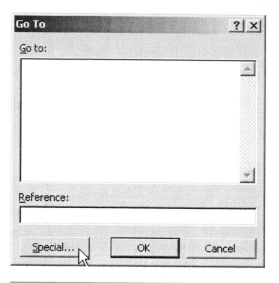

Step	Procedure	Description
❏ Step 3	Hit the Special button.	*We need the Visible Cells Only selection.*

The Go To Special dialog has all sorts of fantastic items.

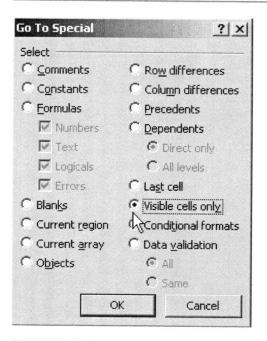

Step	Procedure	Description
❏ Step 4	Select the Visible cells only option and hit OK.	*Your selection now includes only the cells that you can see in your subtotals, and not the detail that lies underneath.*

When you look at the screen, it is difficult to see anything different in the selection, although your screen has changed a bit.

The appearance of the selection on the screen includes some white stripes, indicating that the hidden rows are not included in the selection.

	C	D	E	F
1	**Product**	**Quantity**	**Avg Price**	**Revenue**
3	**Deluxe Widget Total**	480		$11,995.20
6	**Premium Widget Total**	360		$7,316.40
8	**Quality Widget Total**	480		$8,635.20
11	**Widget Total**	480		$8,155.20
12	**Grand Total**	1800		$36,102.00

Step	Procedure	Description
❏ Step 5	From the Edit menu, select Edit→Copy.	
❏ Step 6	Go to a blank cell or worksheet, and hit Edit→Paste special.	*This method pastes just the subtotaled values.*
❏ Step 7	(Optional) Go to Edit→Replace, and replace the word "Total", with nothing.	*Otherwise, the word "Total" repeats on each row. See illustration below.*
❏ Step 8	Choose Values, then hit **OK**.	*The subtotal values are there and underlying details are gone.*

	Product	Quantity	Avg Price	Revenue
14	Product	Quantity	Avg Price	Revenue
15	Deluxe Widget Total	480		$11,995.20
16	Premium Widget Total	360		$7,316.40
17	Quality Widget Total	480		$8,635.20
18	Widget Total	480		$8,155.20
19	Grand Total	1800		$36,102.00

To remove subtotals

It is particularly courteous to remove subtotals that you created in any shared workbooks.

Follow this procedure to remove your subtotals.

Step	Procedure	Description
❏ Step 1	With one cell in the data range selected, choose Data→Subtotals.	*The Subtotals dialog box displays.*
❏ Step 2	Click the **Remove All** button.	*See the illustration on the following page.*

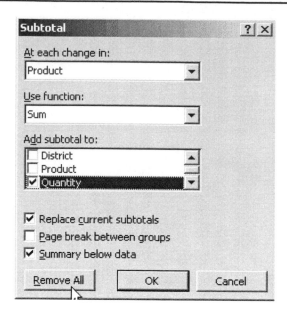

To add additional subtotals

In our example, we could first subtotal by District within Region. To do this, we would sort the data first by Region and then by District. In Excel 2000, you will want to create the subtotals for Region first, then follow these steps to add District subtotals.

Note that the Group and Outline buttons now go from 1 to 4.

1: just the grand total

2: totals by Region

3: by Region and District

4: all of the detail with the totals.

Step	Procedure	Description
☐ Step 1	With one cell in the data range selected, choose Data→Subtotals.	*The Subtotals dialog box displays. See the preceding illustration.*
☐ Step 2	Uncheck the **Replace Current Subtotals** option button.	
☐ Step 3	Choose District for **At each change in:** and hit **OK**.	*You'll now have two sets of subtotals.*

Note that if you add two levels of subtotals, Excel annoyingly adds two Grand Total lines.

Select the entire row and use Edit→Delete to delete the unwanted second Grand Total line.

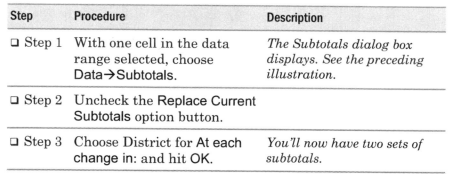

	A	B	C
1	**Region**	**District**	**Product**
2	01	122	Widget
3	01	122	Wodget
4		**122 Total**	
5	01	123	Premium Widget
6	01	123	Quality Wodget
7		**123 Total**	
8	**01 Total**		
9	02	234	Quality Widget
10		**234 Total**	
11	**02 Total**		
12	03	322	Premium Wodget
13		**322 Total**	
14	**03 Total**		
15		**Grand Total**	
16	**Grand Total**		
17			
18			

Subtotals bug in Excel 7.0 (95)

There is a particular problem that can occur when you are creating two levels of subtotals. This problem became evident when Subtotals were introduced in Excel 7.0 for Windows 95. Microsoft developed a workaround in Excel 97, but the workaround requires you to create your subtotals in a particular order..

Here is a simple dataset with sales by Region, Product, and Month.

	A	B	C	D
1	Region	Product	Month	Revenue
2	Central	Widget	Jan	$3,281.00
3	Central	Widget	Feb	$3,451.00
4	Central	Premium Widget	Jan	$6,996.00
5	Central	Premium Widget	Feb	$10,055.00
6	Govt	Premium Widget	Jan	$10,394.00
7	Govt	Premium Widget	Feb	$6,637.00
8	West	Widget	Jan	$2,948.00
9	West	Widget	Feb	$6,921.00
10	West	Premium Widget	Jan	$9,260.00
11	West	Premium Widget	Feb	$4,722.00

In most regions, the company sells two products, a Widget and a Premium Widget. However, in the government region, only the Premium Widgets are sold. Can you foresee the problem around cell B6 when our data is sorted by product within region?

The product column does not change from Premium Widgets as the data switches from the Central Region to the Govt Region. If you apply the subtotals to the product field first, you will get an invalid result.

Here is what happens when you use the incorrect sequence.

If you add subtotals to the product column first, Excel does not add a subtotal between the Central and Govt regions.

1 2 3		A	B	C	D
	1	Region	Product	Month	Revenue
	2	Central	Widget	Jan	$3,281.00
	3	Central	Widget	Feb	$3,451.00
	4		Widget Total		$6,732.00
	5	Central	Premium Widget	Jan	$6,996.00
	6	Central	Premium Widget	Feb	$10,055.00
	7	Govt	Premium Widget	Jan	$10,394.00
	8	Govt	Premium Widget	Feb	$6,637.00
	9		Premium Widget Total		$34,082.00
	10	West	Widget	Jan	$2,948.00
	11	West	Widget	Feb	$6,921.00
	12		Widget Total		$9,869.00
	13	West	Premium Widget	Jan	$9,260.00
	14	West	Premium Widget	Feb	$4,722.00
	15		Premium Widget Total		$13,982.00
	16		Grand Total		$64,665.00

Then, as you add a second set of subtotals by Region, you do get a Govt subtotal.

1 2 3 4		A	B	C	D
	1	**Region**	**Product**	**Month**	**Revenue**
	2	Central	Widget	Jan	$3,281.00
	3	Central	Widget	Feb	$3,451.00
	4	**Central Total**			$6,732.00
	5		**Widget Total**		$6,732.00
	6	Central	Premium Widget	Jan	$6,996.00
	7	Central	Premium Widget	Feb	$10,055.00
	8	**Central Total**			$17,051.00
	9	Govt	Premium Widget	Jan	$10,394.00
	10	Govt	Premium Widget	Feb	$6,637.00
	11	**Govt Total**			$17,031.00
	12		**Premium Widget Total**		$34,082.00
	13	West	Widget	Jan	$2,948.00
	14	West	Widget	Feb	$6,921.00
	15	**West Total**			$9,869.00
	16		**Widget Total**		$9,869.00
	17	West	Premium Widget	Jan	$9,260.00
	18	West	Premium Widget	Feb	$4,722.00
	19	**West Total**			$13,982.00
	20		**Premium Widget Total**		$13,982.00
	21	**Grand Total**			$64,665.00
	22		**Grand Total**		$64,665.00

However, if you click the "3" group and outline button, you get a confusing mess.

1 2 3 4		A	B	C	D
	1	**Region**	**Product**	**Month**	**Revenue**
	4	**Central Total**			$6,732.00
	5		**Widget Total**		$6,732.00
	8	**Central Total**			$17,051.00
	11	**Govt Total**			$17,031.00
	12		**Premium Widget Total**		$34,082.00
	15	**West Total**			$9,869.00
	16		**Widget Total**		$9,869.00
	19	**West Total**			$13,982.00
	20		**Premium Widget Total**		$13,982.00
	21	**Grand Total**			$64,665.00
	22		**Grand Total**		$64,665.00

Note how the Premium Widget Total for the West is in cell D12 of $34 million and is greater than the total sales for the west shown in D19. You can avoid this problem by always creating the subtotals for the least aggregate grouping first.

In this example of the correct method for adding subtotals, the Region totals are always added first.

1 2 3		A	B	C	D
	1	**Region**	**Product**	**Month**	**Revenue**
	2	Central	Widget	Jan	$3,281.00
	3	Central	Widget	Feb	$3,451.00
	4	Central	Premium Widget	Jan	$6,996.00
	5	Central	Premium Widget	Feb	$10,055.00
	6	**Central Total**			$23,783.00
	7	Govt	Premium Widget	Jan	$10,394.00
	8	Govt	Premium Widget	Feb	$6,637.00
	9	**Govt Total**			$17,031.00
	10	West	Widget	Jan	$2,948.00
	11	West	Widget	Feb	$6,921.00
	12	West	Premium Widget	Jan	$9,260.00
	13	West	Premium Widget	Feb	$4,722.00
	14	**West Total**			$23,851.00
	15	**Grand Total**			$64,665.00

The product totals are added next. In Excel 97 and later, Excel will treat the blank cell in column B on the Govt Total row as a reason to insert a product subtotal.

In Excel 95, Microsoft ignored blank lines. No product total would have been added for the Government Premium Widgets.

1 2 3 4		A	B	C	D
	1	**Region**	**Product**	**Month**	**Revenue**
	2	Central	Widget	Jan	$3,281.00
	3	Central	Widget	Feb	$3,451.00
	4		**Widget Total**		$6,732.00
	5	Central	Premium Widget	Jan	$6,996.00
	6	Central	Premium Widget	Feb	$10,055.00
	7		**Premium Widget Total**		$17,051.00
	8	**Central Total**			$23,783.00
	9	Govt	Premium Widget	Jan	$10,394.00
	10	Govt	Premium Widget	Feb	$6,637.00
	11		**Premium Widget Total**		$17,031.00
	12	**Govt Total**			$17,031.00
	13	West	Widget	Jan	$2,948.00
	14	West	Widget	Feb	$6,921.00
	15		**Widget Total**		$9,869.00
	16	West	Premium Widget	Jan	$9,260.00
	17	West	Premium Widget	Feb	$4,722.00
	18		**Premium Widget Total**		$13,982.00
	19	**West Total**			$23,851.00
	20		**Grand Total**		$64,665.00
	21	**Grand Total**			$64,665.00

With this result, you can click on the "3" group and outline button to produce a meaningful summary.

1 2 3 4		A	B	C	D
	1	**Region**	**Product**	**Month**	**Revenue**
	4		**Widget Total**		$6,732.00
	7		**Premium Widget Total**		$17,051.00
	8	**Central Total**			$23,783.00
	11		**Premium Widget Total**		$17,031.00
	12	**Govt Total**			$17,031.00
	15		**Widget Total**		$9,869.00
	18		**Premium Widget Total**		$13,982.00
	19	**West Total**			$23,851.00
	20		**Grand Total**		$64,665.00

In Excel 95, performing the subtotals in the correct order would not eliminate this problem. If your data included adjacent records for the same product from different regions, the automatic subtotals would never work.

Filtering Data

Excel offers two filtering methods. The Advanced Filter has been around forever and is a bit more difficult to use. The Auto Filter was introduced later and is a fantastic method for quickly finding records within data.

Finding records quickly with AutoFilter

Suppose you have a set of data that has invoice data. Each record represents an invoice with customer, product, quantity, and revenue data.

	A	B	C	D	E	F
1	Invoice #	Date	Customer	Product	Qty	Revenue
2	13386	3/29/2002	WLV S.A.	Quality Widget	200	19800
3	13387	3/29/2002	IHH LTD.	Widget	700	62300
4	13388	3/29/2002	CZJ CO.	Quality Widget	200	19800
5	13389	3/29/2002	WLV S.A.	Premium Widget	400	47600
6	13390	3/29/2002	SLW CORP.	Quality Widget	400	39600
7	13391	3/30/2002	WOP INC	Widget	600	53400

It is common to have someone telephone and ask for details about all orders for a particular customer or product. The AutoFilter technique is an excellent way to answer these types of questions.

Finding all records for a particular field

First let's find all the records for a particular customer.

Step	Procedure	Description
❑ Step 1	Be sure that your data has one row of headings at the top and no blank rows or columns.	
❑ Step 2	From the menu, select Data>Filter>AutoFilter.	*Excel adds a dropdown arrow next to each heading.*

	A	B	C	D	E	F
1	Invoice # ▼	Date ▼	Customer ▼	Product ▼	Qty ▼	Revenue ▼
2	13386	3/29/2002	WLV S.A.	Quality Widget	200	19800
3	13387	3/29/2002	IHH LTD.	Widget	700	62300
4	13388	3/29/2002	CZJ CO.	Quality Widget	200	19800
5	13389	3/29/2002	WLV S.A.	Premium Widget	400	47600
6	13390	3/29/2002	SLW CORP.	Quality Widget	400	39600

Step	Procedure	Description
❑ Step 3	Click the dropdown arrow for Customer.	*You will see a list of available customers, plus choices for All, Top 10 and Custom.*

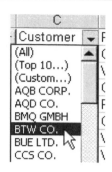

Step	Procedure	Description
❑ Step 4	Select one customer from the list.	*You will see just the records for the selected customer. The other records are still present but have been hidden.*

The drop-down arrow next to Customer turns blue to indicate that the list is filtered by a selection in this column. The row numbers turn blue as well.

	A	B	C	D	E	F
1	Invoice # ▾	Date ▾	Customer ▾	Product ▾	Qty ▾	Revenue ▾
277	13661	5/23/2002	BTW CO.	Premium Widget	100	11900
322	13706	6/1/2002	BTW CO.	Premium Widget	100	11900
499	13883	7/6/2002	BTW CO.	Premium Widget	800	95200
660	14044	8/7/2002	BTW CO.	Premium Widget	700	83300
892	14276	9/23/2002	BTW CO.	Quality Widget	700	69300
949	14333	10/4/2002	BTW CO.	Premium Widget	700	83300
992	14376	10/13/2002	BTW CO.	Quality Widget	700	69300

Finding all records for a different customer

To find records for a different value in a filtered column, it is not necessary to clear the filter. You can simply select a different value from the Customer dropdown.

Finding all records for a particular product

To switch gears and begin filtering by product, you first need to clear the filter on the Customer field.

Step	Procedure	Description
❑ Step 1	Go to the Customer dropdown. Scroll to the top of the list and select (All).	*This clears the original filter. All records will be displayed.*

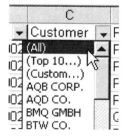

Step	Procedure	Description
❑ Step 2	From the Product dropdown, select Premium Widget.	*Only the records for Premium Widgets will be displayed.*

Filtering based on two fields

If you need to find all the invoices where a particular customer purchased a particular product, this is easy to accomplish.

Step	Procedure	Description
❑ Step 1	Clear any existing filters.	*Select (All) from any dropdown where the arrow is blue*
❑ Step 2	Use the **Product** dropdown to select Quality Widget	*Only the Quality Widget records display.*
❑ Step 3	Use the **Customer** dropdown to select BTW Co.	*The Product filter and Customer filter are joined by an AND – you only see records where the BTW Co ordered Quality Widgets.*

Filtering to find Top 10 (or Top 3%) records

Step	Procedure	Description
❑ Step 1	Go to the **Revenue** dropdown. Scroll to the top of the list and select (All).	*This clears the original filter. All records will be displayed.*

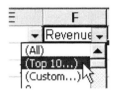

Top 10 only works on numeric fields. Although (Top 10) appears as an option for text fields like Customer, Excel will not show the Top 10 Autofilter after you select Top 10 for a text field.

Step	Procedure	Description
❑ Step 2	From the **Revenue** dropdown, select (**Top 10**).	*The Top 10 AutoFilter dialog displays. You can select either the Top or Bottom n items or the Top or bottom n percent.*

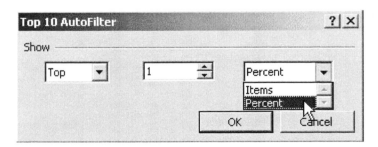

Selecting the Top 1 percent gives you the 1% of the records with the highest revenue. Note that this is based on the number of records and does not respect the 80/20 rule. In this case, we happen to get 10 records (1% of 1004 is 10). The sum of the revenue from these 10 records is 35% of the total revenue.

The Top 10 feature is not *that* smart.

1	Invoice # ▼	Date ▼	Customer ▼	Product ▼	Qty ▼	Revenue ▼
37	13421	4/5/2002	FNM GMBH	Premium Widget	784	93296
154	13538	4/28/2002	XNR INC.	Premium Widget	630	74970
349	13733	6/6/2002	QXB CO.	Premium Widget	704	83776
498	13882	7/6/2002	DPP GMBH	Premium Widget	651	77469
556	13940	7/17/2002	XYV CO.	Premium Widget	672	79968
599	13983	7/26/2002	DDM INC.	Premium Widget	728	86632
710	14094	8/17/2002	NNM S.A.	Premium Widget	672	79968
912	14296	9/27/2002	TLZ CORP.	Premium Widget	624	74256
975	14359	10/9/2002	YBD CORP.	Premium Widget	712	84728
1005	14389	10/15/2002	IIS LTD.	Premium Widget	768	91392

Combining a top 10 revenue filter with a customer filter does not work

Once you see how cool the AutoFilter is, you might hope that you can perform some advanced queries. For example, if I first filter to see all of the records for FNM Co., I might think that I could then ask for just the Top 10 records from that list.

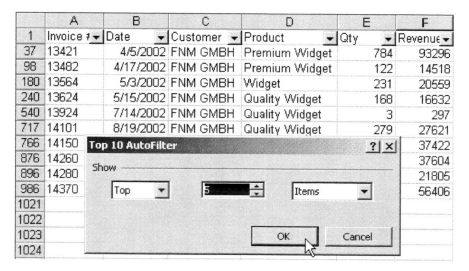

1	Invoice # ▼	Date ▼	Customer ▼	Product ▼	Qty ▼	Revenue ▼
37	13421	4/5/2002	FNM GMBH	Premium Widget	784	93296
98	13482	4/17/2002	FNM GMBH	Premium Widget	122	14518
180	13564	5/3/2002	FNM GMBH	Widget	231	20559
240	13624	5/15/2002	FNM GMBH	Quality Widget	168	16632
540	13924	7/14/2002	FNM GMBH	Quality Widget	3	297
717	14101	8/19/2002	FNM GMBH	Quality Widget	279	27621
766	14150					37422
876	14260					37604
896	14280					21805
986	14370					56406
1021						
1022						
1023						
1024						

Top 10 AutoFilter ? X

Show

[Top ▼] [5 ▲▼] [Items ▼]

[OK] [Cancel]

However, since the results are joined by an AND, you will only get records that are in the top 10 of the entire dataset and for FNM. In this case, that is a single record.

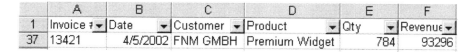

1	Invoice # ▼	Date ▼	Customer ▼	Product ▼	Qty ▼	Revenue ▼
37	13421	4/5/2002	FNM GMBH	Premium Widget	784	93296

Creating somewhat complex queries using the (Custom) AutoFilter

Step	Procedure	Description
❑ Step 1	Go to the **Customer** dropdown and select **(Custom)**.	*The Custom AutoFilter dialog displays.*

Step	Procedure	Description
❑ Step 2	Select all customers whose names start with "A".	*You can specify up to two conditions joined by either AND or OR. You have a variety of choices.*

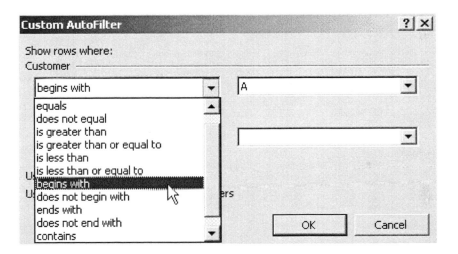

Here you see the results:

	A	B	C	D	E	F
1	Invoice # ▼	Date ▼	Customer ▼	Product ▼	Qty ▼	Revenue ▼
115	13499	4/20/2002	AQB CORP.	Premium Widget	8	952
177	13561	5/3/2002	AQB CORP.	Widget	45	4005
414	13798	6/19/2002	AQD CO.	Quality Widget	162	16038
491	13875	7/4/2002	AQB CORP.	Premium Widget	168	19992
543	13927	7/15/2002	AQB CORP.	Quality Widget	284	28116
664	14048	8/8/2002	AQD CO.	Widget	518	46102
928	14312	9/30/2002	AQB CORP.	Premium Widget	60	7140
943	14327	10/3/2002	AQB CORP.	Widget	190	16910
946	14330	10/3/2002	AQB CORP.	Widget	490	43610
947	14331	10/4/2002	AQB CORP.	Premium Widget	430	51170
984	14368	10/11/2002	AQB CORP.	Premium Widget	420	49980

Filtering dates using Custom AutoFilter

With date fields, it is best to use the Custom AutoFilter. Here, I select all the dates in April, 2002:

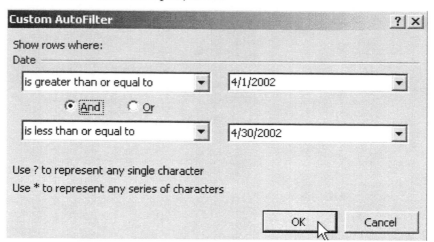

Removing an AutoFilter (removing the dropdown boxes)

To completely remove an AutoFilter, Select Data>Filter>AutoFilter from the menu again. This toggles the AutoFilter to off.

Limitations with AutoFilter

You can only have one AutoFilter per worksheet. If you have a range of Invoices in A1:F1004, and a range of purchase orders in M1:M500, you can only apply the AutoFilter to one range or the other at a time.

One incredibly cool trick with VBA and AutoFilters

VBA is the programming language behind Excel. While you can do incredibly powerful things with VBA (see Veni, Vidi, Vici on page A-31), it is generally beyond the scope of this book.

However, there is one incredibly cool thing that you can do using VBA and AutoFilters that you cannot generally do through the Excel user interface.

Using VBA, you can cause certain fields to not have dropdowns in the AutoFilter. This makes a lot of sense – you may want someone to be able to query by Customer and Product but not by Invoice, Date, Qty, or Revenue. The following macro code will make the dropdowns invisible for all but columns C & D:

For a quick overview of how to run a macro, see http://www.mrexcel.com/tip038.shtml

```
Sub Macro1()
    With Range("A1")
        .AutoFilter field:=1, VisibleDropDown:=False
        .AutoFilter field:=2, VisibleDropDown:=False
        .AutoFilter field:=5, VisibleDropDown:=False
        .AutoFilter field:=6, VisibleDropDown:=False
    End With
End Sub
```

After you run this code, the AutoFilter only offers dropdowns for Customer and Product:

	A	B	C	D	E	F
1	Invoice #	Date	Customer ▾	Product ▾	Qty	Revenue
2	13386	3/29/2002	WLV S.A.	Quality Widget	138	13662
3	13387	3/29/2002	IHH LTD.	Widget	273	24297
4	13388	3/29/2002	CZJ CO.	Quality Widget	172	17028

Using Advanced Filter

The Advanced Filter function pre-dates the AutoFilter. It is more powerful, but also significantly harder to use. However, the Advanced Filter has some cool uses. It remains one of the best ways to extract a unique list of customers from a database of invoice records.

Like the AutoFilter, your data should be set up in list format. Have one row of headings above your data. Make sure each heading is unique. Make sure there are no entirely blank rows or columns in your data.

In addition to your list of data, you may often need to build a small criteria range off to the side of your data. In this area, you will copy headings for certain fields and specify which values you would like to see in the field.

Advanced Filter example 1 – Filter in place

The option to Filter the list in place is very similar to using AutoFilter. Instead of selecting criteria from a dropdown, you must build the criteria off to the side of the data. Here is simple criteria to find all sales of Quality Widgets to WLV S.A.:

H	I
Customer	Product
WLV S.A.	Quality Widget

Step	Procedure	Description
❏ Step 1	Select a single cell in your data range.	
❏ Step 2	From the menu, select Data>Filter>AutoFilter.	*The Advanced Filter window displays.*

Step	Procedure	Description
❑ Step 3	Specify a Criteria range of H1:I2.	
❑ Step 4	Click OK.	*The result shows only the rows that match the criteria. All of the other rows will be hidden.*

	A	B	C	D	E	F
1	Invoice #	Date	Customer	Product	Qty	Revenue
2	13386	3/29/2002	WLV S.A.	Quality Widget	138	13662
84	13426	4/6/2002	WLV S.A.	Quality Widget	234	23166
105	13480	4/16/2002	WLV S.A.	Quality Widget	116	11484
115	13517	4/24/2002	WLV S.A.	Quality Widget	49	4753

To Show All Records Again

From the Menu, select **Data>Filter>Show All**.

Advanced Filter example 2 – Copy to another location

In this example, we would like to get any records for either Premium Widgets or Revenue greater than $90,000. We would like to copy the data to a new section of the worksheet.

Because we want to join the two conditions with an OR, each item in the criteria range should be on a different row.

H	I
Product	Revenue
Premium Widget	
	>90000

Step	Procedure	Description
❑ Step 1	Select a single cell in your data range.	
❑ Step 2	From the menu, select Data>Filter>AutoFilter.	*The Advanced Filter window displays.*

Step	Procedure	Description
☐ Step 3	Click the Radio button for Copy to another location.	
☐ Step 4	Change the Criteria range to include Row 3.	
☐ Step 5	In the **Copy to:** box, specify a blank cell off to the side.	
☐ Step 6	Click **OK**.	*The result is a new data table in K1:P334 with just the matching records.*

	K	L	M	N	O	P
1	Invoice #	Date	Customer	Product	Qty	Revenue
2	13499	4/20/2002	AQB CORP.	Premium Widget	8	952
3	13927	7/15/2002	AQB CORP.	Quality Widget	994	98406
4	14312	9/30/2002	AQB CORP.	Premium Widget	60	7140

Advanced Filter example 3 – Copy only certain fields to another location

In example 2, the Copy to: range was a blank cell, so the results showed all of the fields from the original data table. It is possible to type in a list of headings in the Copy to: range and have the Advanced Filter return only these columns from the data. This method can be used with or without a criteria field.

Let's say that we want to see the Invoice #, Date, and Quantity of all sales of Quality Widgets to the ZMB Co. In the image below, the criteria range is in H2:I2 and the output range is in K1:M1.

	H	I	J	K	L	M
1	Customer	Product		Invoice #	Date	Qty
2	ZMB CO.	Quality Widget				

Step	Procedure	Description
☐ Step 1	From the menu, select Data>Filter>Advanced Filter.	*The Advanced Filter window displays.*

Step	Procedure	Description
☐ Step 3	Click the radio button for Copy to another location.	
☐ Step 4	Change the Criteria range: to stop at I2.	
☐ Step 5	Specify that the Copy to: range includes only columns K:M.	
☐ Step 6	Click OK.	*The result is just the three selected columns for the matching records:*

	K	L	M
1	Invoice #	Date	Qty
2	13412	4/3/2002	53
3	13439	4/8/2002	504
4	13450	4/10/2002	70
5	13472	4/15/2002	252
6	13477	4/16/2002	396
7	13568	5/4/2002	56

Advanced Filter example 4 – Unique records only

The Advanced Filter is a great way to extract a unique list of customers from data.

Step	Procedure	Description
❑ Step 1	Select a single cell in your data range.	
❑ Step 2	From the menu, select Data>Filter>AutoFilter.	*The Advanced Filter window displays.*

Step	Procedure	Description
❑ Step 3	Click the radio button for **Copy to another location.**	
❑ Step 4	In the **List range:**, change both column indicators to **C.**	
❑ Step 5	Clear the **Criteria range:.**	
❑ Step 6	In the **Copy to:** box, specify a single blank cell.	
❑ Step 7	Check the box for **Unique records only.**	
❑ Step 8	Click **OK.**	*The result in K1:K103 is a unique list of all customers who ordered products.*

Advanced Filter example 5 – Conditions created as the result of a formula

Imagine that you wanted to extract all of the records for either Quality Widgets or Premium Widgets for either WLV S.A. or for IHH LTD. Since you have two values in each of two fields, your criteria range grows to four rows.

H	I
Product	Customer
Quality Widget	WLV S.A.
Premium Widget	WLV S.A.
Quality Widget	IHH LTD.
Premium Widget	IHH LTD.

You can imagine that if you had 4 criteria fields each with 2 possibilities, your criteria range would include 2x2x2x2 possibilities or 16 rows.

I once tried to build a criteria range with six fields and each field could be any one of 6-12 values. The combinations were something like 9 x 6 x 12 x 8 x 10 x 7. Literally, this criteria field would have taken 362,880 rows, a ridiculously impossible criteria table to build.

Luckily, there is a good work-around for this that works incredibly well.

It is called **Conditions created as the result of a formula.**

Step	Procedure	Description
❑ Step 1	Leave row 1 of your Criteria range blank and enter a formula in row 2.	*This formula should include a relative reference that refers to the column label or to the corresponding field in the first record.* *All other references in the formula must be absolute references.*
❑ Step 2	To select all orders greater than the average revenue, you would use the formula at right in H2 as the Criteria range.	<table><tr><td>**H**</td><td>**I**</td></tr><tr><td></td><td></td></tr><tr><td colspan="2">=F2>Average($F$2:$F$1020)</td></tr></table>

Note that after you enter this formula, it will evaluate to either a TRUE or FALSE depending on the data in F2. However, as Excel performs the filter, it evaluates every cell in column F instead of just cell F2.

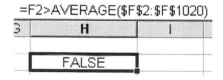

=F2>AVERAGE($F$2:$F$1020)

G	H	I
	FALSE	

Step	Procedure	Description
❏ Step 3	In the **Advanced Filter** box, specify a **Criteria range**: that includes the blank cell H1 and the formula in H2.	*The results will be just the above-average sales, copied to a new location.*

Advanced Filter example 6 – Solving the 362,880 condition problem

In example 5, I mentioned a situation where I wanted to select six to 12 possible selections from six different fields. Using a series of conditions created as the result of a formula will solve this problem.

Step	Procedure	Description
❏ Step 1	Off to the side of your data, build a list of the customers and products that you would like to retrieve.	*In this case, the customer list is in K2:K9 and the product list is in M2:M3.*

=NOT(ISNA(MATCH(C2,$K$2:$K$9,FALSE)))

H	I	J	K	L	M
			Customer		Product
TRUE	TRUE		AQB CORP.		Premium Widget
			AQD CO.		Quality Widget
			BMQ GMBH		
			BTW CO.		
			CCS CO.		
			CDU LTD.		
			DDM INC.		
			DJZ GMBH		

Step	Procedure	Description
❏ Step 2	In Cell H2, enter the following formula: =NOT(ISNA(MATCH(C2, $K$2:$K$9,FALSE)))	*This formula will determine if the customer in C2 is in the list of customers in K2:K9.*
❏ Step 3	In cell I2, enter the following formula: =NOT(ISNA(MATCH(D2, $M$2:$M$9,FALSE)))	*This formula will determine if the product in D2 is in the list of customers in M2:M3.*
❏ Step 4	Select a single cell in your data range.	
❏ Step 5	From the menu, select Data>Filter>Advanced Filter.	*The Advanced Filter window displays.*

Step	Procedure	Description
❏ Step 6	Click the radio button for Copy to another location.	
❏ Step 7	Specify H1:I2 as the Criteria range:.	
❏ Step 8	Specify a blank range in the Copy to: box.	
❏ Step 9	Click OK.	*The results in O1:T92 are the sales to the 8 selected customers for the 2 selected products.*

	O	P	Q	R	S	T
1	Invoice #	Date	Customer	Product	Qty	Revenue
2	13499	4/20/2002	AQB CORP.	Premium Widget	8	952
3	13875	7/4/2002	AQB CORP.	Premium Widget	168	19992
4	13927	7/15/2002	AQB CORP.	Quality Widget	284	28116
5	14312	9/30/2002	AQB CORP.	Premium Widget	60	7140
6	14331	10/4/2002	AQB CORP.	Premium Widget	430	51170

Conclusion

Filters span the continuum. From incredibly simple AutoFilters that can be built with a few mouse clicks to incredibly complex Advanced Filters using multiple criteria built as the result of a formula, they can be used in a myriad of situations.

SUMIF and COUNTIF

SUMIF

SUMIF formulas allow you to quickly total a large number of detail records using one criterion.

SUMIF formulas enable an accounting department to generate a trial balance from their accounting system and paste the records into Excel. Everyday, they can generate a new report that is pasted onto the Data worksheet.

	A	B	C	D	E
1	ACCOUNT	CENTER	DATE	JOURNAL	AMOUNT
2	A315	C28	1/12/02	J52	1099.88
3	A907	C44	1/16/02	J86	7105.07
4	A150	C46	1/29/02	J77	894.51
5	A870	C71	1/25/02	J35	3319.29
6	A481	C35	1/13/02	J25	1251.52
7	A492	C39	1/17/02	J50	8418.6
8	A384	C66	1/11/02	J90	3778.26
9	A236	C16	1/13/02	J28	6817.19
10	A153	C57	1/29/02	J96	3783.18
11	A856	C98	1/27/02	J11	8853.64
12	A152	C82	1/6/02	J15	5616.2
13	A624	C56	1/16/02	J70	7877.35
14	A694	C86	1/21/02	J54	7608.77

The syntax of the SUMIF function is:

=SUMIF(Range containing Account Numbers, Account Number to Match, Range containing Revenue to be summed)

Column C contains a generic SUMIF statement to get the total of Data!Column C for one account.

	A	B	C	D	E	F	G
1	G/L TRIAL BALANCE SUMMARY						
2							
3	Account	Description	Amount				
4	A315	Underapplied Overhead	26302.74	=SUMIF(Data!A:A,Sheet2!A4,Data!E:E)			
5	A481	Shop Supplies	7846.31				

In our particular example, the summary worksheet has many pre-defined accounts set up in a summary. This format allows an accounting department to quickly create complicated summary reports immediately after dropping in new data from their mainframe accounting system.

The formula in cell C4 is:

=SUMIF(Data!A:A,Sheet2!A4,Data!E:E)

This tells Excel: Cruise through all of the cells in column A of the Data worksheet. Any time that the value in column A matches the account shown in A4, sum the corresponding value from column E of the Data sheet.

SUMIF with two criteria

SUMIF generally doesn't work with two criteria.

➤ One workaround is to use a CSE formula (see next chapter).

➤ The other workaround is to build a concatenated key in your list and then use a second concatenated key in the SUMIF formula.

Follow this procedure to use a concatenated key.

Step	Procedure	Description
☐ Step 1	Paste your mainframe data to Excel, then add a new column F.	
☐ Step 2	In column F, enter the formula =A2&B2.	*This joins together the Account and Center numbers.*

	A	B	C	D	E	F
1	ACCOUNT	CENTER	DATE	JOURNAL	AMOUNT	KEY
2	A315	C28	1/12/02	J52	1099.88	=+A2&B2
3	A907	C44	1/16/02	J86	7105.07	A907C44
4	A150	C46	1/29/02	J77	894.51	A150C46
5	A870	C71	1/25/02	J35	3319.29	A870C71
6	A481	C35	1/13/02	J25	1251.52	A481C35
7	A492	C39	1/17/02	J50	8418.6	A492C39

This method using the concatenated key is not as quick as using a single-criteria SUMIF because, after pasting the mainframe data, you generally would have to recalculate the concatenated key formula.

Step	Procedure	Description
☐ Step 3	On your Summary worksheet, enter the formula =SUMIF(Data!F:F,A4&C4, Data!E:E).	*This builds a concatenated value on the fly as the second argument in the SUMIF function.*

	A	B	C	D	E
1	G/L TRIAL BALANCE SUMMARY				
2					
3	Account	Description	Center	Description	Amount
4	A315	Underapplied Overhead		Houston Plant	8073.96
5	A315	Underapplied Overhead	C28	Singapore Plant	1099.88
6					
7	Formula in E4 is:				
8	=SUMIF(Data!F:F,Summary!A4&Summary!C4,Data!E:E)				

COUNTIF

The COUNTIF function has a similar syntax to SUMIF. Instead of summing the cells, COUNTIF counts the number of cells that match a certain criterium.

The keys to the kingdom: CSE

You absolutely CAN learn this formula and use it in your arsenal of data analysis tricks! Even more amazing, your boss can learn it. I've worked for VPs who have learned it!

Imagine that there was a super formula, a brand of formula that could replace ten thousand formulas in a single keystroke. What would you pay for such a formula?

What if Microsoft provided this formula for free? Would that be enough to make you upgrade? You bet!

Let me clue you in on a secret: Microsoft gives you this formula for free, and they've been providing it in every version of Excel since anyone can remember.

CSE is the most powerful formula in Excel, and the least publicized. Microsoft must figure that people can't understand it, won't remember it, or will be intimidated by it.

Using array formulas

Think:
"Can Supercharge Excel".

Back in 1998, I started a campaign to rename these formulas. I call them CSE Formulas.

I'll introduce a very simple example:

You have 10,000 rows of data, which look something like this:

	A	B	C	D	E Unit Price	F Unit Cost
1	Region	Name	Product	Quantity		
2	123	ABC Co.	Premium Widget	120	24.99	15.11
3	125	ComCo	Premium Wodget	480	24.99	15.12
4	134	Achoo	Quality Widget	480	17.99	10.98
5	123	ABC Co.	Quality Wodget	240	17.99	11.07
6	125	ComCo	Widget	240	16.99	10.31
7	134	Achoo	Wodget	240	16.99	10.22

The goal is to find the total of Quantity times the Unit Price for ALL 10,000 rows. Most Excel users would look at the following formula and assume there is no way it could ever work:

=SUM(D2:D10001*E2:E10001)

At first blush, it won't. If you were creative enough to try this formula, Excel would return a #VALUE! Error. So, most budding Excel gurus would do the obvious:

1. Insert a temporary column and enter =D2*E2 in the first data row.
2. Copy it down all 10,000 rows.
3. Do a sum of that column, such as =SUM(G2:G10001).

If you're good, you can accomplish this whole procedure in 30 seconds or less.

The secret? The original formula and other, far more complex formulas, can and do work. But in order to make them work, you must use a very non-intuitive set of keystrokes.

Type your formula:

=SUM(D2:D10001*E2:E10001)

CSE Formulas:

Ctrl+Shift+Enter

Also called:

Array formulas

Now, instead of just hitting Enter, first hold down the Ctrl and Shift keys and then hit the Enter key. Instead of getting a #VALUE! error, you'll get the correct answer.

Look at this: Excel is doing the 10,000 multiplications and totaling them for you! It is a fantastically powerful formula. One single cell – 10,000 calculations.

Lets look at some other cool uses for CSE or Array formulas.

In an earlier chapter, I discussed using SUMIF functions. These functions are excellent if you have only one condition that you need to test. In the data set below, there are quantities of products by Region and Product.

	A	B	C	D	E	F	G	H	I	J
1	**Region**	**Product**	**Qty**							
2	123	ABC	11							
3	234	DEF	15		Region	Total Qty				
4	345	GHI	11		123	389	=SUMIF($A$2:$A$122,E4,$C$2:$C$122)			
5	123	JKL	14		234	424				
6	234	ABC	4		345	393				
7	345	DEF	14			1206				
8	123	GHI	9							
9	234	JKL	17		Product	Total Qty				
10	345	ABC	12		ABC	259	=SUMIF($B$2:$B$122,E10,$C$2:$C$122)			
11	123	DEF	2		DEF	325				
12	234	GHI	14		GHI	292				
13	345	JKL	9		JKL	330				
14	123	ABC	17			1206				
15	234	DEF	11							

It is a straightforward process to create normal SUMIF formulas in F4:F6 to calculate the total by region:

=SUMIF($A$2:$A$122,E4,$C$2:$C$122)

It is also easy to create a formula in E10:E13 that calculates the total by product:

=SUMIF($B$2:$B$122,E10,$C$2:$C$122)

If you want a formula to calculate the total sales for product ABC to Region 123, SUMIF falls short because it cannot handle two conditions. However, a CSE formula can work wonders with two or more conditions.

	E	F	G	H	I	J
2		—*Region* —>				
3	**Product**	**123**	**234**	**345**	**Total**	
4	**ABC**	77	78	104	259	
5	**DEF**	104	113	108	325	
6	**GHI**	79	118	95	292	
7	**JKL**	129	115	86	330	
8	**Total**	389	424	393	1206	
9						
10	Formula in F4:					
11	=SUM(($A$2:$A$122=F$3)*($B$2:$B$122=$E4)*($C$2:$C$122))					

Step	Procedure
❑ Step 1	Type the following formula in cell F4: =SUM(($A$2:$A$122=F$3)*($B$2:$B$122=$E4)*($C$2:$C$122))
❑ Step 2	Hold down Ctrl+Shift while hitting Enter.

The preceding formula uses the Boolean Logic rules (see Remedial reading, page 98). Although this is the fastest formula, you might find the following variation to be more intuitive:

=SUM(IF($A$2:$A$122=F$3,IF($B$2:$B$122=$E4,$C$2:$C$122,0),0))

Copying array formulas

You can copy a CSE formula without having to hold down Ctrl+Shift+Enter.

If your formula from step 1 were a normal (non-CSE) formula, you could simply copy F4 and paste it to F4:H7. Because F4 contains a CSE formula, your paste region must not contain the original copied formula. This requires you to do the extra steps shown here.

You can enter a formula once and then safely use copy and paste without having to hold down Ctrl+Shift+Enter. However, there is one peculiar limitation. You cannot paste a CSE formula into a range that contains a mix of CSE formulas and blank cells. If you attempt to do this, Excel will warn you that you "Cannot change part of an array". This means that you need to follow these steps:

Step	Procedure
❑ Step 1	Type the following formula in cell F4: =SUM(($A$2:$A$122=F$3)*($B$2:$B$122=$E4)*($C$2:$C$122))
❑ Step 2	Copy cell F4.
❑ Step 3	Paste to cells G4:H4.
❑ Step 4	Copy cells F4:H4.
❑ Step 5	Paste to cells F5:H7.

Advanced array formulas

The sample above shows how to extend the concept of SUMIF or COUNTIF to handle two conditions. Array formulas are far more powerful. Literally any Excel function can be incorporated into an array formula. If for some reason you needed to sum all of the sales where the Customer Name is exactly four times as long as the Customer City, you could create an array formula to do this:

=SUM(IF(LEN($A$2:$A$1000)=4*LEN($B$2:$B$1000),$C$2:C$1000,0))

If you needed to know the average number of characters in a column of text:

=AVERAGE(LEN(A2:A1000))

Finding CSE in the help files

I will admit that I had a bad experience with linear algebra during my sophomore year at college. If you want my brain to shut down, simply start talking about arrays. Microsoft chose to call these formulas "Array Formulas". Personally – and I realize I may be biased due to my linear algebra experience – just the name "Array Formula" scares me away.

Further, I also generally found that I would have an occasion to use CSE formulas about once a month. It was really hard to remember the keystroke combination – Ctrl+Shift+Enter – for something that was used rather infrequently. I've started a campaign to rename array formulas as "CSE Formulas" in an effort to help remind you that you need to hold down Ctrl+Shift+Enter with the formula.

If you choose to read the Microsoft Help sections on the topic, you will need to search for "Array Formulas".

Array formulas and their impact on overhead

Array formulas are pretty slick, but be aware that they take a lot of overhead. A few array formulas here or there are okay, but do not attempt to run an entire report from array formulas. I once had a client with 50,000 rows of data. They had 2,000 products being carried in 30 stores. They had a great idea to create a two-dimensional array to show sales by store and product. They had their 30 stores going across columns B:AE and a few hundred products going down column A. I attempted to produce a report with 3,000 array formulas. Each array formula had to analyze 50,000 rows of data. Needless to say, the recalculation time on that report was hours instead of seconds. In this case, using a single Pivot Table allowed the same report to be created in seconds.

Pivot tables

My assumption with this book is that you have the basics of Excel down. However, pivot tables are so important, I will spend a few pages discussing the basics of what a pivot table can do and how they work.

Back in 1993, Lotus came out with a fantastic product called Improv. It was a whiz-bang analysis tool that could let you easily create cross-tabs with your data. This was functionality that I had been pitching to Pansophic for their EZIQ product. Lotus had solved the problem and it was available for just $99. I bought a copy the day I saw it demonstrated.

Critics will say that Microsoft steals good ideas from their competitors. Excel 95 took the Lotus Improv concept and renamed it a Pivot Table. They included it, for free, with Excel 95. That put an end to Lotus' stand-alone product.

Pivot tables were the greatest things since sliced bread. A single pivot table could replace dozens of =DSUM formulas. In reality, most Excel users didn't have the patience to learn the DSUM function, so pivot tables really gave analysts a whole new tool.

Pivot table capabilities

A pivot table lets you create a "cross-tab" analysis.

Our sample data contains 1,000 rows of sales data by Region, Product, and Year. The basic premise of a pivot table is that it lets you create a "cross-tab" analysis. This is an analysis where, say, all of the regions are going down the rows of the left column and all of the products are going across the first row of each column. At the intersection of each region and product, you see the sales for that region and product.

Sample data

	A	B	C	D	E	
1	Region	Product	Year	Sales	Profit	
2	West	ABC	2002	67000	24120	
3	East	ABC	2004	36000	14760	
4	West	ABC	2003	7000	3220	
5	East	ABC	2004	54000	25380	
6	West	ABC	2002	38000	15960	
7	West	ABC	2002	44000	19800	
8	East	GHI	2003	71000	26270	
9	Central	GHI	2003	83000	29050	
10	Central	DEF	2002	46000	22540	

Here is a pivot table summarizing the 1000 rows of data.

Pivot table

Sum of Sale	Product ▼			
Region ▼	ABC	DEF	GHI	Grand Total
Central	5383000	5541000	6146000	17070000
East	4936000	5862000	6378000	17176000
West	5036000	5025000	5974000	16035000
Grand Total	15355000	16428000	18498000	50281000

To rearrange a pivot table, click on the gray field name in the pivot table, and drag to a new location.

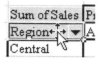

Once you have the pivot table created, you can drag field headings to change the look of the pivot table. In the table below, I dragged Region to go across the top, products to go down the side, and added a new field, Year, to go down the side.

Sum of Sales		Region ▾			
Year ▾	Product ▾	Central	East	West	Grand Total
2002	ABC	2051000	1788000	1441000	5280000
	DEF	1620000	1805000	1215000	4640000
	GHI	1850000	1940000	1906000	5696000
2002 Total		5521000	5533000	4562000	15616000
2003	ABC	2076000	1653000	1950000	5679000
	DEF	2063000	2673000	1946000	6682000
	GHI	2513000	2147000	1657000	6317000
2003 Total		6652000	6473000	5553000	18678000
2004	ABC	1256000	1495000	1645000	4396000
	DEF	1858000	1384000	1864000	5106000
	GHI	1783000	2291000	2411000	6485000
2004 Total		4897000	5170000	5920000	15987000
Grand Total		17070000	17176000	16035000	50281000

It is common in data analysis to want to prepare a report for each regional manager, but not to want the regional managers to see results from the other regions. In this case, we would use something called the Page Field of the pivot table.

When I initially moved Region to the top, the pivot table defaulted to showing (All) regions, which gave the Region field a dropdown. Using the dropdown, I can quickly select any region to create a report tailored to each manager.

In this image, I moved Year to go across the top, left Product along the side, and moved Region up to the page field section.

Region	Central ▾			

Sum of Sales	Year ▾			
Product ▾	2002	2003	2004	Grand Total
ABC	2051000	2076000	1256000	5383000
DEF	1620000	2063000	1858000	5541000
GHI	1850000	2513000	1783000	6146000
Grand Total	5521000	6652000	4897000	17070000

How to create a pivot table

Version variations:

In Excel 95 and 97, there were four steps to the Pivot Table Wizard. In Excel 2000 and 2002 (XP), there are only three steps to the wizard, as a "Layout" button in Step 2 replaced the third step.

For compatibility, I always walk you through initially using the Layout button.

Note that it is possible to use an Access table or query as the source for your data, which is a really cool thing.

Start with a rectangular range of data in list format. It is really important for every row to have a non-blank heading on a single row. Excel uses these headings to refer to your data, so they should be meaningful. Headings need to be unique.

Step	Procedure	Description
❑ Step 1	Select a single cell inside the range and select Data→Pivot Table and Pivot Chart Report.	*The Pivot Table Wizard launches.*
❑ Step 2	In Step 1 of the Pivot Table Wizard, indicate that your data is coming from a Microsoft Excel list or database.	*Although your data could come from Access, for this book we focus on using data inside of Excel.*

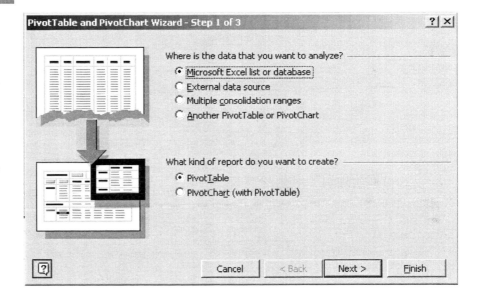

Step	Procedure	Description
❑ Step 3	Click Next to go to Step 2 of the Wizard. Specify the range of data that you want to use.	*If you selected a single cell in a range of data in List Format, the range specified here is correct.*

Step	Procedure	Description
❑ Step 4	Click Next.	*In Excel 95/97, Step 3 of 4 – the Layout step – displays. In Excel 2000 & later, click the Layout button in Step 3 of 3 to see the Layout screen.*

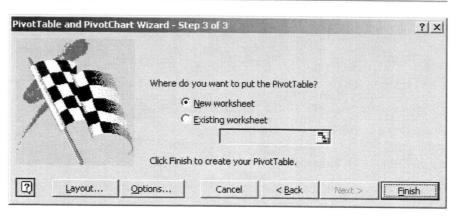

Step	Procedure	Description
❑ Step 5	Press the **Layout** button.	*The Layout dialog displays.*

In the Layout dialog box, there are four white areas on the left, named Page, Row, Column, and Data. On the right, you have several gray buttons, each representing a field in your data.

Shortcut Keys:

To move a field to the Data, Column, Row, or Page section of the pivot table, click on the field and hit the **Alt** *key plus the* **D, C, R,** *or* **P** *key, respectively.*

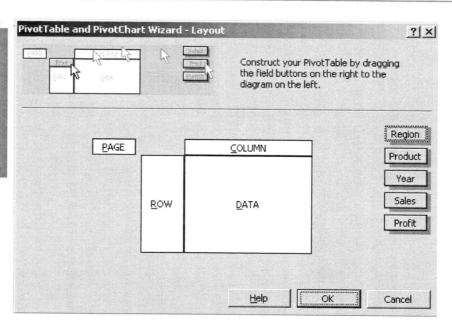

If you are using Excel 95 or 97, you must build your pivot table in this manner. If you are using Excel 2000 or XP, you can either use this method or build it directly on the worksheet.

To build the pivot table in layout view, you simply drag the gray field buttons and drop them onto the corresponding sections of the white box. In our case, we want to start with a table showing Regions down the side, Products across the top and Sales as the data field.

Step	Procedure	Description
❑ Step 6	Drag the Products field and drop it on the area labeled Column.	*Optionally, select Products and hit* Alt+C.
❑ Step 7	Drag the Region field and drop it on the area labeled Row.	*Optionally, select Region and hit* Alt+R.
❑ Step 8	Drag the Sales field and drop it on the area labeled Data.	*Optionally, select Sales and hit* Alt+D. *The name field changes from Sales to Sum of Sales. See Note at left.*

When you drop Sales on the Data section, the gray field name box changes from "Sales" to "Sum of Sales". Always check this. If it contains "Count of Sales", you have one or more non-numeric entries in your Sales column. See the Intermediate tips, tricks, and troubleshooting section on page 54 for help on handling this.

PivotTable and PivotChart Wizard - Layout ? X

Construct your PivotTable report by dragging the field buttons on the right to the diagram on the left.

PAGE   Product COLUMN

Region   Region
                Product
Region   Sum of Sales   Year
                Sales
ROW   DATA   Profit

Help   OK   Cancel

Step	Procedure	Description
❑ Step 9	Click the OK button in Excel 2000 / XP or the Next button in Excel 95 / 97 to continue.	*Your Layout dialog should look like the one above before you continue.* *The Layout dialog closes and you return to Step 3 of 3 (Step 4 of 4 in Excel 95/97).*

In the final step of the wizard, Excel defaults to putting the pivot table on a new sheet. I prefer to put the pivot table on the existing sheet, off to the right of the data.

PivotTable and PivotChart Wizard - Step 3 of 3 ? X

Where do you want to put the PivotTable?

⊙ New worksheet

○ Existing worksheet

Click Finish to create your PivotTable.

Layout...   Options...   Cancel   < Back   Next >   Finish

Step	Procedure	Description
❑ Step 10	Select either the New worksheet or Existing worksheet option.	*If you select Existing worksheet, you can click where you want the Pivot table to display on the worksheet.* *If you do not select a location on your worksheet, the Pivot Table displays in the upper left corner of a new worksheet.*
❑ Step 11	Click Finish.	*Your pivot table appears in the selected area.*

Things to note about pivot tables

> ➤ If you are on a worksheet with a pivot table, the pivot table toolbar will appear.

> ➤ If you actually select a cell within the pivot table, then the PivotTable Field List will appear. In Excel 2000, the field list appears in a "larger" version of the pivot table toolbar. In Excel 2002, they have moved the field list to its own separate floating window as shown below.

Prior to Excel 2000, Excel did not offer the PivotTable Field List. In Excel 95 or 97, you would have to click the Layout Wizard button on the Pivot Table toolbar to add new fields to the pivot table.

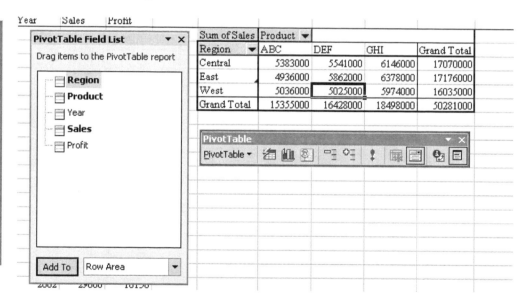

Intermediate tips, tricks, and troubleshooting

Change a pivot table on the fly

The beauty of pivot tables is that you can change them on the fly.

> ➤ For Excel 97, hit the layout button in the pivot table toolbar.

> ➤ For Excel 2000, you can drag a gray field button to a new position (you can drag off the chart to remove the field). You can also drag new fields from the PivotTable Field List.

"Count of Sales" instead of "Sum of Sales".

This is annoying and is the most common problem with pivot tables. If your sales column has a single non-numeric field, Excel assumes that you have non-numeric data and offers to count it instead of summing it. The right thing to do is to go find the non-numeric data and fix it. However, the "count problem" can happen even if you have one empty cell in the column.

If you notice this problem while you are in layout view, double-click the **Count of Sales** button to bring up the PivotTable Field dialog. Change the **Summarize by:** list box from **Count** to **Sum** and click **OK**. Refer to the following image for more detail.

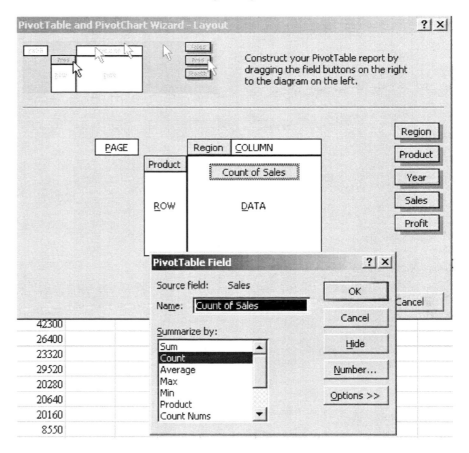

Error messages

"You can not change this part of a PivotTable report" or "You cannot change, move a part of, or insert cells in a Pivot Table".

If you are really doing Guerilla Data Analysis, you are thrilled with the results of the pivot table – after all, you just eliminated a dozen =DSUM() formulas, and want to take that data somewhere else. You have already tried to slice and dice the data, only to be told, "You can not change this part of a pivot table report."

If you really just want the summarized data, then do this:

Highlight the entire pivot table, press **Edit→Copy**, and then press **Edit→Paste Special→Values→OK**.

How to delete a pivot table

In order to delete a pivot table, you must first delete all of the columns that hold the pivot table. Otherwise, you get the "You can not change, move a part of, or insert cells in a pivot table" message. Try deleting all of the columns if you get this message.

Double-click any pivot table cell to zoom in

You can double-click any data cell in a pivot table. Excel creates a new worksheet and copies all of the records from the original data that were used to calculate that total.

Region	Central ▼			
Sum of Sales	Year ▼			
Product ▼	2002	2003	2004	Grand Total
ABC	2051000	2076000	1256000	5383000
DEF	1620000	2063000	1858000	5541000
GHI	1850000	2513000	1783000	6146000
Grand Total	5521000	6652000	4897000	17070000

Double-click on the cell with the total sales for ABC product in 2004 (see above). Excel creates a summary of all the records that make up $1,256,000 (see the following page).

	A	B	C	D	E
1	**Region**	**Product**	**Year**	**Sales**	**Profit**
2	Central	ABC	2004	87000	40020
3	Central	ABC	2004	21000	8610
4	Central	ABC	2004	76000	31920
5	Central	ABC	2004	54000	22680
6	Central	ABC	2004	33000	13860
7	Central	ABC	2004	84000	37800
8	Central	ABC	2004	42000	15540
9	Central	ABC	2004	99000	43560
10	Central	ABC	2004	82000	40180
11	Central	ABC	2004	5000	1950
12	Central	ABC	2004	27000	12960
13	Central	ABC	2004	34000	13940
14	Central	ABC	2004	19000	7410
15	Central	ABC	2004	54000	19980
16	Central	ABC	2004	14000	5320
17	Central	ABC	2004	96000	39360
18	Central	ABC	2004	60000	29400
19	Central	ABC	2004	13000	5330
20	Central	ABC	2004	15000	5250
21	Central	ABC	2004	53000	21730
22	Central	ABC	2004	20000	9600
23	Central	ABC	2004	88000	42240
24	Central	ABC	2004	64000	29440
25	Central	ABC	2004	6000	2580
26	Central	ABC	2004	21000	7770
27	Central	ABC	2004	89000	36490
28					

Sum=1256000

Pre-specify sequence of pivot table

To our running sample data, I've added a customer name and transaction date. If I create a pivot table showing sales by customer, the default sort is alphabetized by customers. This default sort order can be changed as you create the pivot table.

Step	Procedure	Description
❑ Step 1	In the Layout View, double-click the Customer field.	*The PivotTable Field dialog displays.*

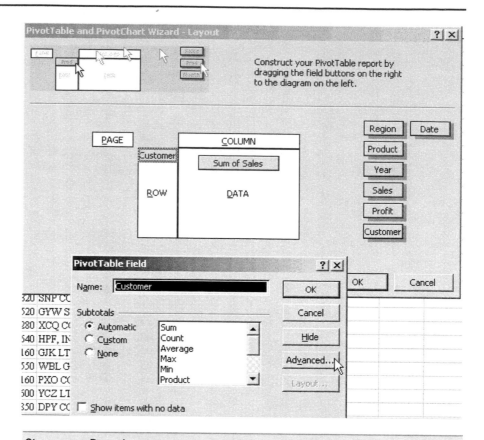

Step	Procedure	Description
❑ Step 2	Click the **Advanced...** button.	*The PivotTable Field Advanced Options dialog displays.*

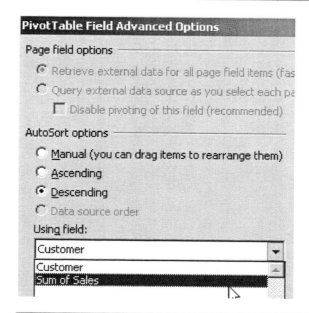

Step	Procedure	Description
❑ Step 3	Select **Descending**.	*Descending is under AutoSort.*

Step	Procedure	Description
❑ Step 4	From the field list dropdown, change the default from Customer to Sum of Sales.	*The resulting Pivot Table is sorted with the largest customer in terms of revenue at the top of the list.*

Sum of Sales	
Customer ▼	Total
FWP GMBH	700000
VSB S.A.	678000
NDN CO.	667000
FLG CO.	661000
MER GMBH	659000
NOF S.A.	658000
UJM, INC.	650000
YDQ S.A.	637000
TTK CO	637000

Manually specify sequence of pivot table

Sometimes you need the results of a pivot table to be in a certain order, and neither alphabetic nor by revenue will work. I've seen situations where the convention was to always report the East region first, the Central region second, and the West region third.

Step	Procedure	Description
❑ Step 1	Create the pivot table with the default sort.	

	I	J	K	L	M
		Drop Page Fields Here			
	Sum of Sales	Region ▼			
	Customer ▼	Central	East	West	Grand Total
	FWP GMBH	155000	210000	335000	700000
	VSB S.A.	385000	210000	83000	678000

Step	Procedure	Description
❑ Step 2	Click in Cell J4 and type East.	*This is the cell that currently has the heading for Central.*
❑ Step 3	Hit Enter.	*Excel automatically reorders the regions so that East is first. Central, which was formerly first, moves to the next position.*

Sum of Sales	Region ▼			
Customer ▼	East	Central	West	Grand Total
FWP GMBH	210000	155000	335000	700000
VSB S.A.	210000	385000	83000	678000

Report top 10 customers per region

Top 10 reports make a great quickie report for the boss. You can easily specify that your pivot table should only include the Top 10 (or 15 or 20) customers.

Step	Procedure	Description
☐ Step 1	In the Layout View, double-click the Customer field.	*The PivotTable Field dialog displays.*

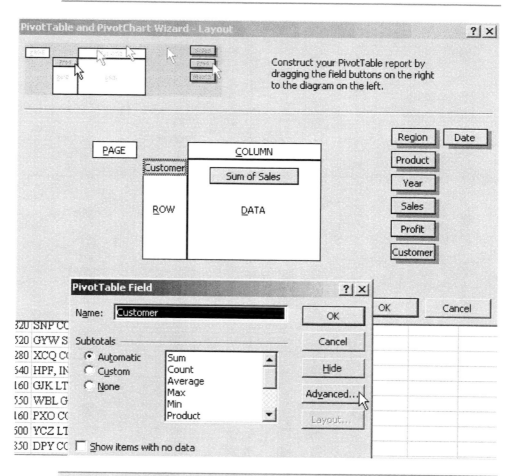

Step	Procedure	Description
☐ Step 2	Click the Advanced... button.	*The PivotTable Field Advanced Options dialog displays.*

On the right side of the PivotTable Field Advanced Options dialog, there are settings for "Top 10 Auto Show".

While this has nothing to do with the annual event held in Detroit each year, it is a useful tool.

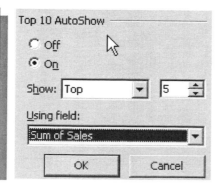

Step	Procedure	Description
❑ Step 3	Indicate that you only want to see the Top 5 using Sum of Sales.	*The Top 10 AutoShow settings are on the right side of the Pivot Table Field Advanced Options dialog.*

Region	Central ▼
Sum of Sales	
Customer ▼	Total
MEF CORP.	420000
FPJ CO.	387000
VSB S.A.	385000
AOX S.A.	314000
YIO, INC.	311000
Grand Total	1817000

Step	Procedure	Description
❑ Step 4	Hit OK.	*The resulting pivot table lets you quickly see the top 5 customers for any region.*

Automatically group dates by month, quarter, year

Step	Procedure	Description
❑ Step 1	Create the pivot table report with the Date field as one of the fields in the pivot report.	
❑ Step 2	In the pivot table, right click the Date heading. Select Group and Show Detail, then Group...	*The Grouping dialog displays.*

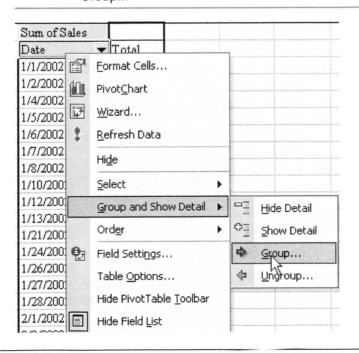

If your underlying data contains transaction dates, Excel allows you to easily consolidate the date fields up to a month or year.

Step	Procedure
❏ Step 3	In the Grouping dialog, indicate that you want to group the Dates by Months and Quarters. Hit OK.

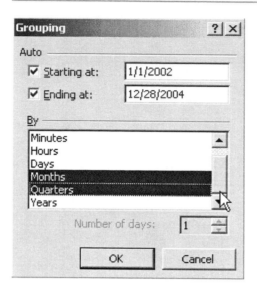

For your first grouping selection (Months), Excel actually changes the Date field to aggregate by month. If you choose a second grouping level (in this case, Quarters), Excel adds a new field to the Pivot Table Field List showing Quarters.

Sum of Sales		
Quarters ▼	Date ▼	Total
Qtr1	Jan	3866000
	Feb	4078000
	Mar	4889000
Qtr2	Apr	4210000
	May	3883000
	Jun	4365000
Qtr3	Jul	3553000
	Aug	3972000
	Sep	4164000
Qtr4	Oct	4487000
	Nov	4595000
	Dec	4219000
Grand Total		50281000

Quarters:

Excel always assumes that Jan through March represent Quarter One. For anyone who works in a company where your fiscal year ends on a date other than December 31st, you are basically out of luck. For most U.S. retailers, Quarter 1 is actually February through April.

Excel offers a myriad of grouping criteria, from seconds up to years. I once received a telephone call from someone who wanted Excel to group by weeks, which is not currently an option. In this case, you would need to add a temporary column to your data with a date calculation to calculate the week – the Automatic Grouping will not help.

Calculated items and calculated fields: useful, but not perfect

It has been a dozen years since my attempts to calculate a Gross Profit Percent on the total lines was foiled by Pansophic's EZIQ. We've come a long way since then. Excel can now calculate that elusive GP %, but it still fails at other complex calculations in pivot tables.

Microsoft really gets your hopes up, offering not one, but TWO methods of calculating in a pivot table. Neither method works the way I would like it to 100% of the time, but both might come in handy at some point.

Calculated items

You cannot add a calculated field to a pivot table that has been grouped. Right click any field that has been grouped, select Group and Outline, then Ungroup.

A calculated item offers one method for grouping two or more values along one dimension of a pivot table. In the data that I have been using, the company sells three products – ABC, DEF, and GHI. Let's say the Hardware division of the company is responsible for ABC and DEF. We want to show a total of those two items. It is possible to add a calculated item that actually creates a fourth value along the Product dimension.

Step	Procedure	Description
❑ Step 1	Click the field where you want to add the calculated item in the pivot table.	*In this case, that would be the Product field.*
❑ Step 2	On the Pivot Table toolbar, click the **Pivot Table** button. Select **Formulas**, then **Calculated Item**.	*The Insert Calculated Item in "Product" dialog displays.*

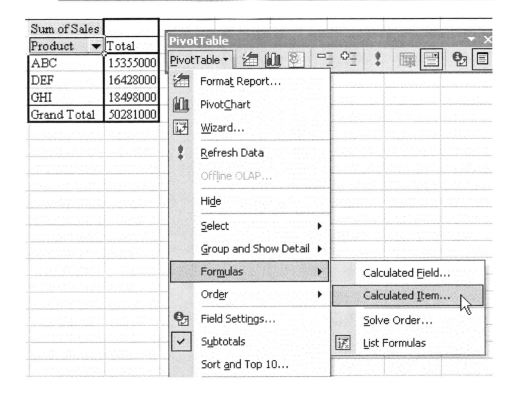

Step	Procedure	Description
❑ Step 3	In the Insert Calculated Item dialog, type a name for the item, then type the formula =ABC+DEF.	*We used Hardware in this example.*
❑ Step 4	Click the **Add** button, and then click **OK**.	*Excel adds a new item to the list of products.*

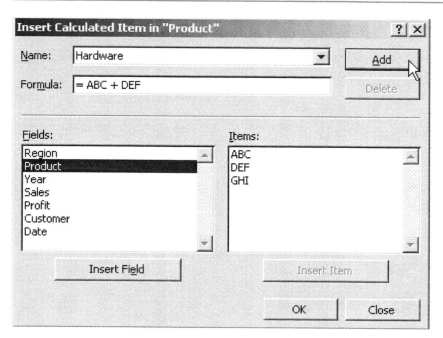

I have several complaints. First, the new item is added to the end of the list instead after DEF. Second, Excel has added Hardware to the Grand Total, which is absolutely wrong.

Examine the results of adding a *calculated item* to the product dimension.

Sum of Sales	
Product ▼	Total
ABC	15355000
DEF	16428000
GHI	18498000
Hardware	31783000
Grand Total	82064000

There are two annoying problems. First, the new item is added to the end of the list instead immediately after DEF. Second, Excel has added Hardware to the Grand Total, which produces a result that is absolutely wrong.

The only way to make any use out of the calculated item is to turn off the display of the hardware components ABC and DEF:

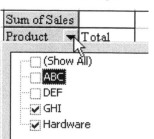

Calculated fields

While a calculated item adds a new value to a single dimension, a calculated field will add a new field that can be reported in the data section of a pivot table.

Step	Procedure	Description
❑ Step 1	With any cell in your pivot table selected, click the Pivot Table button in the Pivot Table toolbar.	
❑ Step 2	Select Formulas→Calculated Field...	*The Insert Calculated Field dialog displays.*

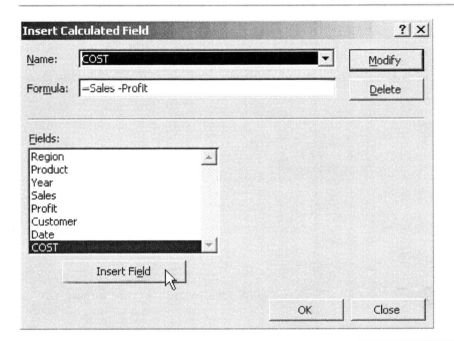

Step	Procedure	Description
❑ Step 3	In the Insert Calculated Field dialog, type a name for the field and a formula. Click Insert Field.	*The resulting pivot table now has a new calculated field.*

Note that the calculation operates on the Total lines. First, the pivot table calculates the Total Sales for a region, then the Total Profit for a region, and subtracts the Total Profit from Total Sales to get Total Cost.

Data	Region	Total
Sum of Sales	Central	17070000
	East	17176000
	West	16035000
Sum of Profit	Central	7187540
	East	7175540
	West	6674530
Sum of COST	Central	9882460
	East	10000460
	West	9360470
Total Sum of Sales		50281000
Total Sum of Profit		21037610
Total Sum of COST		29243390

This makes Calculated Fields fine for any operation that follows the associative law of mathematics – this is the rule that says you can do the calculation in any order without changing the results.

The calculation for Gross Profit Percent does work correctly, although the default label of "Total Sum of GP Pct" is a little misleading.

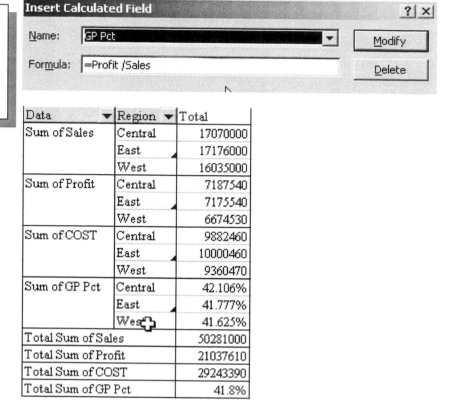

Data	Region	Total
Sum of Sales	Central	17070000
	East	17176000
	West	16035000
Sum of Profit	Central	7187540
	East	7175540
	West	6674530
Sum of COST	Central	9882460
	East	10000460
	West	9360470
Sum of GP Pct	Central	42.106%
	East	41.777%
	West	41.625%
Total Sum of Sales		50281000
Total Sum of Profit		21037610
Total Sum of COST		29243390
Total Sum of GP Pct		41.8%

Calculated fields fail when you need Excel to perform the calculation at the detail level and then SUM the results of those calculations.

An example would be if you needed to calculate the average sales price for a series of products and then sum the averages. Instead, Excel averages the sum on the total line.

Pivot table Q & A

Q: Can I show both Sales and Profit in the Table?

A: Yes – you can show both sales and profit. Drag profit to the data area of the pivot table. You get the following default view, which, in my opinion, is the least useful view of the data. Within each Product going down the side, you get a line for Sum of Sales and a line for Sum of Profit. At the end of the table, you have two rows: a Grand total for Sales and a Grand Total for Profit.

		Region ▼			
Product ▼	Data ▼	Central	East	West	Grand Total
ABC	Sum of Sales	5383000	4936000	5036000	15355000
	Sum of Profit	2279410	2079150	2126500	6485060
DEF	Sum of Sales	5541000	5862000	5025000	16428000
	Sum of Profit	2327830	2448440	2096460	6872730
GHI	Sum of Sales	6146000	6288000	5974000	18408000
	Sum of Profit	2580300	2647950	2451570	7679820
Total Sum of Sales		17070000	17086000	16035000	50191000
Total Sum of Profit		7187540	7175540	6674530	21037610

Q: Why does Excel choose the stupidest possible view of the data when I select two data fields?

A: I may know a lot about Excel, but I have no intelligent theories about why Microsoft would choose this ugly presentation as their default view.

Q: Can I show two data fields in a different manner and make it look better?

A: Yes, you can make it look better, but it is incredibly subtle. On the worksheet, grab the Data field with your mouse and drag it up ¼ of an inch so it is to the left of the Region field button. The mouse cursor does change, but it is barely perceptible.

As you start to drag, the blue rectangle appears going down the rows. When you see the blue rectangle change to appear going across the top of the rows, drop the field and you will have this view of the data, which I also generally hate. Here, they keep Sales together and Profit together, but then tack the total of Sales and the total of Profit on to the extreme far right.

	Data ▼	Region ▼							
	Sum of Sales			Sum of Profit			Total Sum of Sales	Total Sum of Profit
Product ▼	Central	East	West	Central	East	West		
ABC	5383000	4936000	5036000	2279410	2079150	2126500	15355000	6485060
DEF	5541000	5862000	5025000	2327830	2448440	2096460	16428000	6872730
GHI	6146000	6288000	5974000	2580300	2647950	2451570	18408000	7679820
Grand Total	17070000	17086000	16035000	7187540	7175540	6674530	50191000	21037610

Now that you have the hang of moving the Data field, try moving the Region field to the left of the Data field. This produces something that is still not very useful.

Region ▾	Data ▾						Total Sum of Sales	Total Sum of Profit
	Central		East		West			
Product ▾	Sum of Sales	Sum of Profit	Sum of Sales	Sum of Profit	Sum of Sales	Sum of Profit		
ABC	5383000	2279410	4936000	2079150	5036000	2126500	15355000	6485060
DEF	5541000	2327830	5862000	2448440	5025000	2096460	16428000	6872730
GHI	6146000	2580300	6288000	2647950	5974000	2451570	18408000	7679820
Grand Total	17070000	7187540	17086000	7175540	16035000	6674530	50191000	21037610

Finally, drag the Data field to the left of the Product field. In my opinion, this is the most useful appearance with two fields, but I would still prefer to have the Sales Grand Total to appear with the Sales rows instead of appearing at the end of the data.

		Region ▾			
Data ▾	Product ▾	Central	East	West	Grand Total
Sum of Sales	ABC	5383000	4936000	5036000	15355000
	DEF	5541000	5862000	5025000	16428000
	GHI	6146000	6288000	5974000	18408000
Sum of Profit	ABC	2279410	2079150	2126500	6485060
	DEF	2327830	2448440	2096460	6872730
	GHI	2580300	2647950	2451570	7679820
Total Sum of Sales		17070000	17086000	16035000	50191000
Total Sum of Profit		7187540	7175540	6674530	21037610

Q: Now that I have two data fields on the pivot table, how do I remove one?

A: Up until Excel 2002 (XP), you could use the Layout button on the toolbar to bring up the Layout Dialog and drag the Profit field out of the white area. In 2002, click the dropdown arrow on the gray Data button on the pivot toolbar and uncheck Sum of Profit.

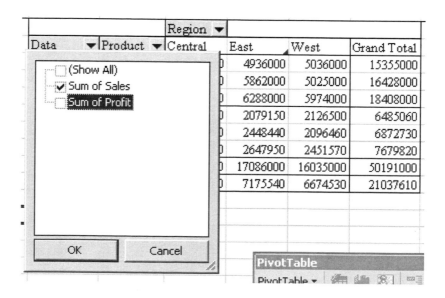

Q: When I change a number in the original data, does it automatically show up in the pivot table?

A: No! You have to hit the red exclamation point on the pivot table toolbar to rebuild the pivot table.

Q: Some of my data is missing. If I have a product that is only sold by one region, the totals for the other region will be blank instead of zeroes. Why?

A: There is no way to fix this in Excel 95. In Excel 97 and later, there is a PivotTable Options dialog box. You can access this in the second-to-the-last step of the Pivot Table Wizard, or through the Pivot Table toolbar. On the toolbar, click the PivotTable button and then choose Table Options from the dropdown list. On the right side of the PivotTable Options, check the box for "For Empty Cells, show:" and enter 0 in the text box for this option.

Sum of Sales	Region ▼			
Product ▼	Central	East	West	Grand Total
ABC	5383000	4936000	5036000	15355000
Avacado			83000	83000
DEF	5541000	5862000	5025000	16428000
GHI	6063000	6288000	5974000	18325000
Grand Total	16987000	17086000	16118000	50191000

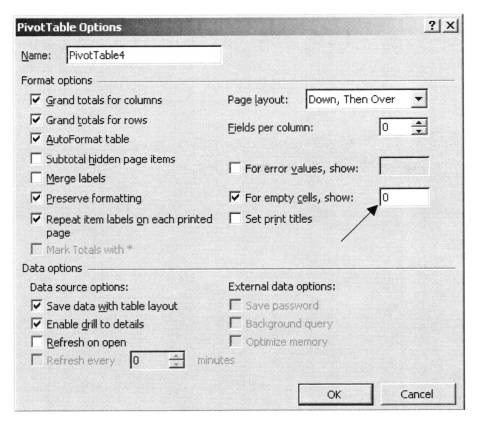

Q: What if I don't want a grand total column or a grand total row?

A: After all of our frustrations with the strange location for grand totals in the question above, it is sometimes easier to simply remove the grand total row or columns. On the PivotTable Options dialog, uncheck the Grand Total for Rows or Grand Total for Columns.

Q: How can I handle the annoying "outline view" when there are two or more column fields?

A: The outline view (shown on the next page) is extremely annoying. Pivot tables are fantastic at solving the classic data processing "control break" coding. You can add a new level of subtotals with the drag of a mouse instead of dozens of COBOL statements. However, the outline view presentation has problems.

Excel offers a truly non-useful method of displaying the data. They use a classic "outline" view where the outermost field is filled in only when it changes. Here is a pivot table by Year, Product, and Region. The value of "2002" only appears once and it is blank for all the remaining year 2002 summary rows. The value of "ABC" appears once and the two cells below it are blank.

I don't know why Microsoft is so hung up on this outline view. If you are going to use the results of a pivot table for anything else (by using Paste Special Values), you really want the values "2003" to appear in every summary row to which it applies.

Year	Product	Region	Sum of Sales	Sum of Profit
2002	ABC	Central	2051000	858000
		East	1788000	770680
		West	1441000	597710
	ABC Total		5280000	2226390
	DEF	Central	1620000	692060
		East	1805000	767960
		West	1215000	506380
	DEF Total		4640000	1966400
	GHI	Central	1850000	803640
		East	1940000	811170
		West	1906000	780080
	GHI Total		5696000	2394890
2002 Total			15616000	6587680
2003	ABC	Central	2076000	876490
		East	1653000	679800
		West	1950000	837670
	ABC Total		5679000	2393960
	Avacado	West	83000	29050
	Avacado Total		83000	29050
	DEF	Central	2063000	855580

There have been many complaints about this feature. Microsoft attempted to fix it in Excel 2000, but missed the point entirely. You can double-click the Year field, click the Layout button and switch between something called Tabular view and an Outline view, but what Microsoft calls Outline view is just as bad.

Year	Product	Region	Sum of Sales	Sum of Profit
2002				
	ABC			
		Central	2051000	858000
		East	1788000	770680
		West	1441000	597710
	ABC Total		5280000	2226390
	DEF			
		Central	1620000	692060
		East	1805000	767960
		West	1215000	506380
	DEF Total		4640000	1966400
	GHI			
		Central	1850000	803640
		East	1940000	811170
		West	1906000	780080
	GHI Total		5696000	2394890
2002 Total			15616000	6587680
2003				
	ABC			
		Central	2076000	876490
		East	1653000	679800
		West	1950000	837670
	ABC Total		5679000	2393960

There is no good way to solve this problem. My standard response is to take the summary data to a new worksheet and to use Data→Subtotals. This involves the following steps:

Step	Procedure	Description
❑ Step 1	Remove all totals from the pivot table.	*Use the Table Options to turn off grand totals by row.*
❑ Step 2	Double-click the Year field, and change the Subtotals option to None.	
❑ Step 3	Double-click the Product field, and change the Subtotals option to None.	

Step	Procedure	Description
❑ Step 4	Copy the data section of the pivot table.	

Year ▼	Product ▼	Region ▼	Data ▼ Sum of Sales	Sum of Profit
2002	ABC	Central	2051000	858000
		East	1788000	770680
		West	1441000	597710
	DEF	Central	1620000	692060
		East	1805000	767960
		West	1215000	506380
	GHI	Central	1850000	803640
		East	1940000	811170
		West	1906000	780080
2003	ABC	Central	2076000	876490
		East	1653000	679800
		West	1950000	837670
	Avacado	West	83000	29050
	DEF	Central	2063000	855580
		East	2673000	1117450
		West	1946000	818790
	GHI	Central	2430000	1004870
		East	2057000	909720
		West	1657000	707510
2004	ABC	Central	1256000	544920
		East	1495000	628670
		West	1645000	691120
	DEF	Central	1858000	780190
		East	1384000	563030
		West	1864000	771290
	GHI	Central	1783000	742740
		East	2291000	927060
		West	2411000	963980

Step	Procedure	Description
❑ Step 5	In a new section of the worksheet, select Edit→ Paste Special→ Values→OK.	

Step	Procedure	Description
❑ Step 6	In the new data, highlight the range with the missing data.	

Year	Product	Region	Sum of Sa	Sum of Profit
2002	ABC	Central	2051000	858000
		East	1788000	770680
		West	1441000	597710
	DEF	Central	1620000	692060
		East	1805000	767960
		West	1215000	506380
	GHI	Central	1850000	803640
		East	1940000	811170
		West	1906000	780080
2003	ABC	Central	2076000	876490
		East	1653000	679800
		West	1950000	837670
	Avacado	West	83000	29050
	DEF	Central	2063000	855580
		East	2673000	1117450
		West	1946000	818790
	GHI	Central	2430000	1004870
		East	2057000	909720
		West	1657000	707510
2004	ABC	Central	1256000	544920
		East	1495000	628670
		West	1645000	691120
	DEF	Central	1858000	780190
		East	1384000	563030
		West	1864000	771290
	GHI	Central	1783000	742740
		East	2291000	927060
		West	2411000	963980

Step	Procedure	Description
❑ Step 7	Hit Ctrl+G.	*This brings up the Go To dialog.*
❑ Step 8	Click the Special button in the lower left. Select Blanks and hit OK.	

Step	Procedure	Description
❑ Step 9	While all the blank cells are selected, type an = sign. Hit the **Up Arrow** key, and then hit **Ctrl+Enter**.	*This fills in all of the missing cells with the data from the cell above.*

Year	Product	Region	Sum of Sa	Sum of Profit
2002	ABC	Central	2051000	858000
2002	ABC	East	1788000	770680
2002	ABC	West	1441000	597710
2002	DEF	Central	1620000	692060
2002	DEF	East	1805000	767960
2002	DEF	West	1215000	506380
2002	GHI	Central	1850000	803640
2002	GHI	East	1940000	811170
2002	GHI	West	1906000	780080
2003	ABC	Central	2076000	876490
2003	ABC	East	1653000	679800
2003	ABC	West	1950000	837670
2003	Avacado	West	83000	29050
2003	DEF	Central	2063000	855580
2003	DEF	East	2673000	1117450

Step	Procedure	Description
❑ Step 10	Re-select the entire range that you selected in Step 6.	*You need to change the formulas from Step 8 to Values; however, you cannot use Paste Special on a non-contiguous range.*
❑ Step 11	Hit **Edit→Copy** and then **Edit→Paste Special→Values**.	*You now have a useful range of summary data that can be used for further data analysis.*

INDIRECT and OFFSET functions

There are several functions in Excel that don't do much calculating, but rather allow you to write very flexible formulas. This chapter covers two very obscure functions.

INDIRECT function

When you use INDIRECT, you are telling Excel that instead of listing a cell address to be used every time, you want Excel to calculate the cell reference on the fly.

You can build dynamic spreadsheets using the INDIRECT function. Its syntax, which is very simple, can take either of two forms:

=INDIRECT("text that evaluates to a valid A-1 cell reference")

or:

=INDIRECT("text that contains a valid R1C1 cell reference",FALSE)

Here is a very trivial example. This formula returns the value that is in cell B10.

=INDIRECT("B10")

The power of INDIRECT comes into play when you use concatenation to build the cell reference. Let's say that you have a workbook with twelve monthly worksheets: JAN, FEB, MAR, and so on. There are a variety of calculations on each worksheet, but the final result always appears in cell D24 of each month's worksheet. When the workbook is opened, you want the results on the summary page to automatically return the results from cell D24 of the current month.

Custom cell formatting:

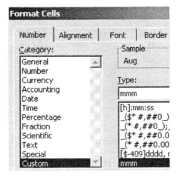

On the number tab of the Format Cells dialog, select Custom from the Category listbox, then type any valid numeric format in the Type: *box.*

Without using INDIRECT, you might have to change the formula each month from =JUL!D24 to =AUG!D24 then =SEP!D24, etc. Using INDIRECT, you can do this automatically. Here are the steps to create a simple summary page:

The formula to return today's date is =TODAY(). It returns a date in your default date style. Look in cell B1 below – mine returned August 1, 2002 in the U.S. mm/dd/yyyy format. In cell B2, I've entered the same formula, but used the custom number format of "mmm" to return a three-digit month name.

	A	B	C	D	E	F	G
1	Today's Date:	8/1/2002	=TODAY()				
2		Aug	=TODAY(), with a custom number format of "mmm"				
3		Aug	=TEXT(B1,"mmm")				
4		Aug!D24	=B3&"!D24"				
5	Answer:	147852	=INDIRECT(B4)				
6	Answer:	147852	=INDIRECT(TEXT(TODAY(),"mmm")&"!D24")				

In cell B3, I've used the text function to simulate setting a custom number format. The syntax is =TEXT(any number,"Number Format"). In this case, I typed, =TEXT(B1, "mmm") to return a 3 digit month abbreviation.

In cell B4, I use the concatenation operator (&) to join together the sheet name with the cell that I want to address. =B3&"!D24" returns a valid A1-style reference of Aug!D24.

In cell B5, I use =INDIRECT(B4) to finally get the result that I wanted. As you open this spreadsheet in a new month, cell B5 automatically returns the value from the current month's spreadsheet.

Of course, you can nest all of these functions together into a single formula as I have done in cell B6:

=INDIRECT(TEXT(TODAY(),"mmm")&"!D24")

Advanced INDIRECT

What if you want your summary to return every detail line from the current month's spreadsheet?

	A	B	C	D
1	AUGUST FORECAST			
2				
3				
4	**Division**	**Hardware**	**Software**	**Total**
5	Central	1,529,000	183,000	1,712,000
6	East	1,416,000	169,000	1,585,000
7	West	390,000	46,000	436,000
8	**USA**	3,335,000	400,000	3,735,000
9	Canada	933,000	111,000	1,044,000
10	**N. America**	4,268,000	511,000	4,779,000
11				
12	U.K.	984,000	118,000	1,102,000
13	Germany	1,021,000	122,000	1,143,000
14	France	445,000	53,000	498,000
15	Italy	469,000	56,000	525,000
16	Spain	1,294,000	155,000	1,449,000
17	Belgium	1,286,000	154,000	1,440,000
18	**EMEA**	5,499,000	658,000	6,157,000
19				
20	Australia	753,000	90,000	843,000
21	Japan	497,000	59,000	556,000
22	**Asia Pacific**	1,250,000	149,000	1,399,000
23				
24	**TOTAL**	11,017,000	1,318,000	12,335,000

With the example shown above, you would have to enter a different INDIRECT function for each cell, which could be very tedious.

The CELL function allows you to determine the address of a particular cell. This seems like a very useless function, until you combine it with the INDIRECT function.

=CELL("Address",B5) returns "$B$5"

=CELL("row",B5) returns 5

=CELL("col",B5) returns 2, because B is the second column on the worksheet

To create a current month view, I've entered a formula of =TODAY() in cell C1 and formatted it with a "mmm" numeric format. In cell B5, enter this formula:

=INDIRECT(TEXT($C$1, "mmm")& "!"&CELL("address",B5))

	A	B	C	D
1	CURRENT MONTH:		Aug	
2				
3				
4	**Division**	**Hardware**	**Software**	**Total**
5	Central	1,529,001	183,000	1,712,001
6	East	1,416,000	169,000	1,585,000
7	West	390,000	46,000	436,000
8	**USA**	3,335,001	400,000	3,735,001
9	Canada	933,000	111,000	1,044,000
10	**N. America**	4,268,001	511,000	4,779,001

In cell B5, this evaluates to =INDIRECT("Aug!$B$5").

As you copy to C5, the CELL function changes and Excel evaluates:

=INDIRECT("Aug!$C$5")

This formula can be entered once and copied to all cells on the Summary worksheet.

Using INDIRECT with an array formula

There are two styles of array formulas. One style is discussed in the chapter on CSE formulas. The other style allows you to select a range of cells and enter a single formula that returns several answers; those answers then fill the range of cells. Our Summary worksheet is a place where this might be appropriate. Select the range of cells B5:D10. Type this formula:

=INDIRECT(TEXT($C$1, "mmm")& "!B5:D10")

Do not just hit **Enter**. Hold down the **Ctrl** and **Shift** keys while hitting **Enter**. This will enter a single formula that eliminates the need to use the CELL function.

Using INDIRECT as an Argument for Another Function

You can use INDIRECT to replace a cell reference in another function. For example, the following formula returns the sum of cells B5:B35 on the current month's worksheet:

=SUM(INDIRECT(TEXT(TODAY(),"mmm")& "!B5:B35"))

Instead of using the CELL function shown in our example on the prevous pages, you could use the Index() function. Let's say that your monthly worksheets have the days of the month running from A5:A35.

	A	B
1	SEPTEMBER	
2	Daily Sales Target	
3		
4	Day	Sales
5	1	20,096
6	2	35,193
7	3	28,741
8	4	6,322
9	5	22,322
10	6	31,967
11	7	32,161
12	8	46,096
13	9	15,612
14	10	19,935
15	11	39,580
16	12	14,258
17	13	45,419
18	14	23,741
19	15	5,516
20	16	29,838
21	17	10,612
22	18	11,645
23	19	32,225
24	20	17,387

⊮ ◄ ► ⊮ \Sep / Oct / N

	A	B	C	D	E	F	G	H
1	Today:	9/7/2002	=TODAY()					
2	Day:	7	=DAY(B1)					
3								
4	Today's Goal:	32,161	=INDEX(INDIRECT(TEXT(B1,"mmm")&"!A5:B35"),B2,2)					

Your Summary worksheet would have a function to get the current day in cell B1. In cell B2, use the =DAY(B1) function to return the day of the month. This indicates which relative row in A5:B35 corresponds to today. The function in B4 to return today's goal would be:

=INDEX(INDIRECT(TEXT(B1, "mmm")& "!A5:B35"),B2,2)

While we are covering really non-intuitive, seemingly useless functions, let's talk through the OFFSET function.

OFFSET Function

OFFSET is a funky way to specify a range of cells.

The OFFSET function can be used as an argument anywhere you would like to specify a range of cells. For example, instead of =SUM(B7:E7), you could build a formula of =SUM(OFFSET(B7,0,0,1,4)).

Here are the five arguments of OFFSET:

=OFFSET(1,2,3,4,5)

Where:

1 = Start from this cell reference.

2 = Go down this many rows to define the upper left cell of the range.

3 = Go right this many columns to define the upper left cell of the range.

4 = The final range should be this many rows high.

5 = The final range should be this many columns wide.

Here is a practical example:

	A	B	C	D	E	F	G	H
1	Customer: ABC Company							
2	Through Month: June							
3								
4	Customer	Jan	Feb	Mar	Apr	May	Jun	Jul
5	AAA Co.	26	31	28	33	30	27	26
6	ABC Co.	30	29	28	32	29	26	24
7	BCD Corp.	28	29	29	31	30	27	25

We want to sum the months from January through the month shown in C2 for the customer in C1.

=SUM(OFFSET(A4,MATCH(C1,A5:A99,FALSE),1,1, MATCH(C2,B4:M4,FALSE)))

Let's break that very confusing formula into pieces:

=SUM	
OFFSET(A4,	Start at A4.
MATCH(C1,A5,A99,FALSE),	Go down two rows.
1,	Go right one column.
1,	Range is one row high
MATCH(C2,B4:M4,FALSE)	and six columns wide.
)	Close the OFFSET.
)	Close the SUM.

The OFFSET function is particularly useful for setting up a dynamic range name. If you have a worksheet with a contiguous section of cells, you can use the OFFSET function in the Insert Names Define dialog to have the range name grow or shrink to fit the entries that are present each day.

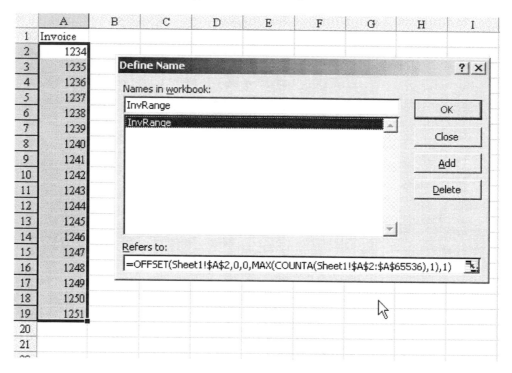

Remedial reading

Hopefully, all of these tricks are old hat for anyone using Excel regularly. However, all of these items are beyond the average new Excel user.

Relative, absolute, and mixed references

This exercise will help you understand the difference between relative- and absolute-referenced formulas.

By default, formulas entered in Excel use relative references.

Step	Procedure	Description
❑ Step 1	Create a spreadsheet like the one below:	

	A	B	C	D
1	Product	Unit Cost	Quantity	Total
2	Premium Widget	24.99	120	=B2*C2
3	Premium Wodget	24.99	480	
4	Quality Widget	17.99	480	
5	Quality Wodget	17.99	240	
6	Widget	16.99	240	
7	Wodget	16.99	240	

Step	Procedure	Description
❑ Step 2	Enter this formula in D2: =B2*C2	
❑ Step 3	Copy this formula down to cell D3.	*Note that the formula changes to:* =B3*C3.

B3 and the C3 are both called **relative** references.

Excel's default of creating formulas with relative references allows you to enter a formula once and copy it to thousands of cells. Sometimes, this will not produce the desired results and we need an absolute reference.

Step	Procedure	Description
❑ Step 1	Create a spreadsheet like the one below:	

	A	B	C	D	E
1				**Mark-Up:**	25%
2	Product	Cost	Retail		
3	Premium Widget	20	25		
4	Quality Widget	10			
5	Widget	9			

Step	Procedure	Description
❑ Step 2	Enter this formula in C3: =B3*(1+E1)	
❑ Step 3	Copy this formula down to cell C4.	*You get the wrong result. The formula changes to:* *=B4*(1+E2).*

As a formula is copied, the various reference types behave in the following ways:

➤ relative (B3)
  changes

➤ absolute ($E$1)
  does not change

➤ mixed (B$1)
  column changes

➤ mixed ($B1)
  row changes

In this case, you want the formula to ALWAYS reference the mark-up percentage in cell E1. The type of reference you need here is called an **absolute** reference. To make a reference absolute, use the $ sign before the column letter and the row number. Try it:

=B3*(1+$E$1)

In this case, B3 is a relative reference and needs to change as the formula is copied. $E$1 is an absolute reference and does not change when copied.

There are two other kinds of references that hold constant either the row or the column when you copy the formula to other cells. Some examples of mixed references:

B$1 allows the column to change, but not the row

$B1 allows the row to change, but not the column

Cell referencing tips

Use the F4 key to toggle through the reference types.

As you are entering a formula, you can type the dollar signs, or better yet, use the **F4** key. Type a reference such as B1, then hit the **F4** key to change the reference type. You'll note that the **F4** key, when hit repeatedly, toggles through the following reference types:

=B1

=$B$1

=B$1

=$B1

Use the End key to "ride the range"

Use the End key to toggle the status bar End indicator.

If you have a contiguous range of data, you can quickly move to the last row by hitting the End key on your keyboard, and then the Down Arrow key.

Hit End and then release it to toggle the End indicator in the status bar at the bottom-right of your application window.

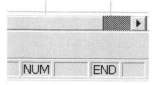

The End and Arrow keys can be used in any direction. In general, after hitting the End key and any Arrow key, you are taken to the non-blank cell at the next boundary between blank and non-blank cells.

	A	B	C	D	E	F	G
85	01	123	Premium Widget			24.99	A
86	03	322	Premium Widget			24.99	B
87	02	234	Quality Widget			17.99	B
88							
89	031	122	Widget			16.99	A
90	01	122	Wodget			16.99	A
91	03	322	Premium Wodget			24.99	B

Using the graphic above, the following actions occur in response to hitting the End and Arrow keys:

Cell Pointer In:	Keystrokes:	Cursor Goes To:	Why
A85	End, Down	A87	Last filled row before blank row
A87	End, Right	C87	Last filled column before blank column
C87	End, Right	F87	Next filled column to right of C87
F87	End, Down	F89	Next filled row below G87
F89	End, Down	F91	Last filled row in range
F91	End, Down	F65536	Last row on the worksheet
F65536	End, Left	A65536	Border of worksheet
A65536	End, Up	A91	Last row with data in Column A

Nesting formulas

You can write long formulas. Any place where you would normally enter a cell reference, you can put another function or formula. You can nest a SUM formula into an IF statement, as shown:

=IF(SUM(A1:A5)>10, "Yes","No")

IF functions

The IF function is a great tool for making decisions in your formulas:

=IF(Some Condition that is True or False, Formula if True, Formula if False)

Nested IF statements

You cannot nest more than seven levels of IF statements. If you need to nest eight or more levels, use a VLOOKUP formula instead.

Using AND and OR in IF statements

Use the =AND or the =OR as the condition of an IF statement to create a column that tells you which cities are capital cities in the state, as follows:

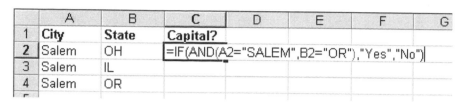

	A	B	C	D	E	F	G
1	City	State	Capital?				
2	Salem	OH	=IF(AND(A2="SALEM",B2="OR"),"Yes","No")				
3	Salem	IL					
4	Salem	OR					

Copy the formula down, and when A2 is Salem and B2 is OR, you'll see Yes; otherwise, you'll see No.

Use Boolean logic facts

Here are the True/False facts:

AND Facts	OR Facts
True * True = True	True + True = True
True * False = False	True + False = True
False * False = False	False + False = False

Using Boolean logic allows you to use this formula instead of the AND and OR formulas shown above:

=IF((A2="Salem")*(B2="OR"), "Yes", "No")

Use the & sign to concatenate text and numbers

You can use the Ampersand (&) to concatenate text and numbers

As shown in the following example, the calculation column contains this formula:

=A2*A2

	A	B	C
1	Number	Calculation	Result
2	1	1	="The Square Root of "&B2&" is "&A2
3	2	4	The Square Root of 4 is 2
4	3	9	The Square Root of 9 is 3
5	4	16	The Square Root of 16 is 4

Page Setup forces reports to fit

Use File→Page Setup options to force an analysis to fit to one page wide. If you have 10,000 rows of data in 12 columns, change the Page Setup, Page tab to Fit To 1 Page Wide. Delete the value in the Tall box to keep Excel from trying to fit your 10,000 rows onto one page. Your data font size is reduced to fit based on the width of your columns.

Manual page breaks are ignored when you use this tip. Instead, you can follow these steps:

1. Set to Fit to: to 1 page(s) wide by (blank) tall.

2. Hit Print Preview.

3. Hit Page Setup. The Adjust to % now displays the correct % to fit all columns to the page.

4. Hit the radio button to use Adjust to:.

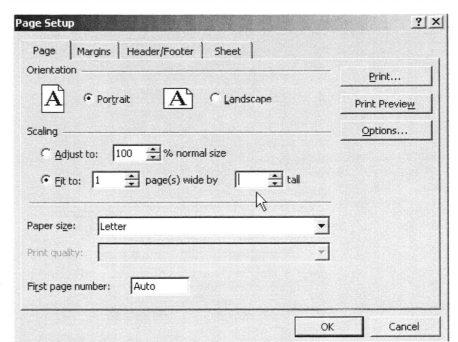

Text manipulation formulas

Formulas that clean up, change, or extract text:

Formula:	Provides:
=LEFT(A1,2)	The first two leftmost characters in cell A1
=RIGHT(A1,2)	The last two rightmost characters in cell A1
=MID(A1,3,2)	The third and fourth characters of cell A1; the 3 denotes the character starting position and the 2 denotes how many characters (moving to the right) to return
=LEN(A1)	The number of characters in the value of cell A1
=TRIM(A1)	Removes any spaces from in front of or behind the value in cell A1, and also any extra spaces between words so that only one space remains between any words
=LOWER(A1)	Copies and converts text in A1 to be all lower case
=UPPER(A1)	Copies and converts text in A1 to all upper case
=PROPER(A1)	Copies and converts text in A1 to all proper case. This method fails for names such as McDonald (it returns Mcdonald) and addresses such as PO Box (it returns Po Box).
=FIND("x",A1)	Returns the position of the character "x" in cell A1. This is great when used in combination with =MID. See the following example.

Combining the MID and FIND formulas helps you extract information such as an account number from text that was not previously broken down.

	A	B
1	Company	Account
2	XYZ Corporation Acct 12345	=MID(A2,FIND("Acct",A2)+5,5)
3	ABC Corporation Acct 23456	
4	Main Street, Inc. Acct 34567	

Date handling

Excel stores dates and times as the number of days since January 1, 1900. For instance, August 15, 2002 is stored as 37483.00. The time is stored as a fraction of a day. Noon is represented as 0.5, and 6:00 am is stored as 0.25.

It is best to use Excel dates and format the cell using Format→Cells to display the date properly.

Type the following into a cell in Excel and hit Enter; then format the cell as a number with 10 decimals:

8/15/2002 3:35 pm

The returned number is: 37483.6493055556

If you have a column of "fake dates" (dates formatted as text that you cannot properly format as dates), you can use Data→Text to Columns to convert the data to real dates:

Step	Procedure
❏ Step 1	Highlight the range of text dates.
❏ Step 2	Choose from the menu, Data→Text to Columns.
❏ Step 3	Choose Fixed Width, Next.
❏ Step 4	Remove any vertical delimiter lines by double clicking them. Click Next.
❏ Step 5	Select Format = Date. Hit Finish.

The following formulas assume that both the date and time are entered into cell A1.

Formula:	Provides:
=NOW()	Returns the present time and date. Whenever your workbook is updated, the value returned changes.
=TODAY()	Returns the date (only) for today. Whenever your workbook is updated, the value returned changes to reflect the current day.
=YEAR(A1)	Returns the year of the date in cell A1.
=MONTH(A1)	Returns the month of the date in cell A1, as a value of 1 through 12.
=DAY(A1)	Returns the day of the month in cell A1, as a value of 1 through 31.
=DATE(YEAR,MONTH,DATE)	This formula converts the date you use to a year, month, and date.

As you can see here, the =DATE function is cool.

This formula is particularly helpful after you've done a Text-to-Columns operation on data that was previously formatted as text. Suppose you have the month in A1, the day in B1, and the year in C1. Just type:

=DATE(C1,A1,B1)

This formula is *very* cool, because even if you have 13 as your month, Excel figures it out.

Now, suppose that you want to figure out a date three months from today. In cell A1, type:

=TODAY()

In any other cell, type:

=DATE(YEAR(A1),MONTH(A1)+3,DAY(A1))

If you type this formula on December 20, 2002, it is equivalent to typing =DATE(2002,15,20) or asking Excel to return the 20th day of the 15th month of 2002. Excel correctly figures out March 20, 2003.

I told you it was cool.

Quickly see Sum/Average of a range

The status bar at the bottom of the Excel window can quickly show you the total of a range of cells. If you have someone on the phone and they need to know a total, you can find it without entering a formula. Simply highlight the range with your mouse, then read the sum from the status bar. If you need to total non-contiguous cells, select one with the mouse, then hold down the Ctrl key and continue to click on the other cells to be summed.

If you right-click the status bar, you can change the Sum to an Average, Min, Max, Count, or Count Numeric.

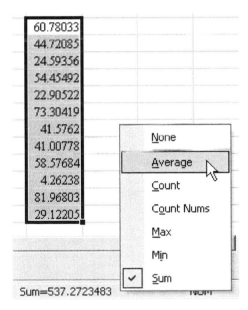

Rank values without sorting

Sometimes you need to know the Number One sales representative, but you cannot sort the data. The RANK formula ranks the values within a list:

	A	B	C	D
1		Sales	Rank	
2	**East Division**			
3	Bob Hart	1,093,206	=RANK(B3,B$3:B$20)	
4	Pat Finnan	1,257,813	2	
5	Jake Dvorak	930,572	10	
6	Kevin Purcell	954,365	9	
7	John Conmy	1,021,061	6	
8	Jerry Holloway	1,021,061	6	
9				
10	**Central Division**			
11	Bill Murphy	1,079,813	5	
12	Wendy Strom	897,258	11	
13	Lori Sampsel	1,002,117	8	
14	Terry Bowman	1,239,527	3	
15				
16	**West Division**			
17	Chuck Shafer	863,724	14	
18	Gwen Rousseau	1,267,565	1	
19	Emily Liggett	877,422	13	
20	Marilyn Paparodis	894,132	12	

Note that if there is a tie in the ranking, as in B7 and B8, Excel assigns both of those values the same rank; in this case, 6; and there is no value with a rank of 7. If you absolutely *need* to have a Rank 6 and a Rank 7, you can get around this limitation by using this formula instead:

=RANK(B3,B$3:B$20)+COUNTIF(B$3:B3,B3)-1

This formula assigns a lower ranking to the first entry that is tied, and a higher number to the second entry that is tied.

Customizing Any Chart Feature with a Right-Click

You can customize absolutely every component of a chart by right-clicking the item and choosing the Format pop-up menu.

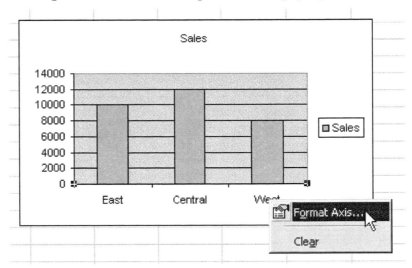

> ➤ Click between the bars to format the plot area (white looks best for a black-and-white printer)

> ➤ Click a data point once to format the data series

> ➤ Click a bar a second time to format the data point

> ➤ Format either the axis, the title, the legend, the gridlines, or the data labels.

You have incredible control to customize a chart once you create it.

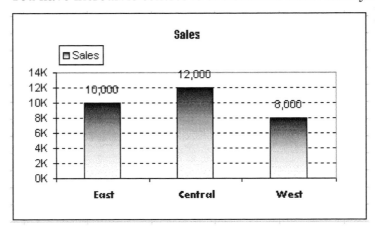

Introduction to Excel functions

Every beginning Excel class covers two functions – SUM() and AVERAGE(). Excel users can get pretty far with just those two basic functions. Even in this book, I've only managed to mention 34 functions – barely 10% of the 340+ functions available within Excel.

A frequent request at MrExcel.com is for a complete printed list of all of the Excel functions. In the Appendix at the end of this section, I have provided just such a list.

There are two professions whose members are classic users of Excel – accountants and engineers. I will accept that most accountants will never have a need to use BESSELI or most of the 38 other engineering functions, but there are still cool functions scattered throughout every section of this list.

I encourage you to occassionally skim through the entire list of 342 functions and select a few that look interesting for investigation. Excel help provides an example for nearly every function listed here (a couple are only here for Lotus compatibility and are not documented in help).

Before launching into the complete list of 342 functions, here is a random sampling of the cool stuff that you can do with various obscure functions.

Predict your car loan payment with PMT()

When it comes time to shop for your next car or house, you can use the simple loan payment calculator to predict the car payment.

	A	B	C	D
1	Price	18500		
2	Term	48	Months	
3	Rate	6.50%		
4	Payment	$438.73	=PMT(B3/12,B2,-B1)	

Use =PMT(Annual Percentage Rate/12,# of Months,-Purchase Price) to calculate a monthly car or house payment.

Round prices up with CEILING()

To round prices up to the nearest nickel or quarter or $5, use the CEILING() function.

	A	B	C	D
1	Cost	Markup	Price	
2	1.99	2.49	=CEILING(B2,0.05)	
3	2.31	2.89	2.90	
4	9.25	11.56	11.60	
5	3.43	4.29	4.30	

Use =CEILING(Number to Round, Significance to Round up to).

Convert between units of measurement with CONVERT()

If you can't remember how to convert Farenheit to Celsius or how many teaspoons are in a tablespoon, the Convert function can help.

	A	B	C	D	E	F
1	From	Units	New Unit	Result		
2	4.2	mi	km	=CONVERT(A2,B2,C2)		
3	2	yr	day	730.5		
4	24	hr	sec	86400		
5	78	F	C	25.56		
6	1	tbs	tsp	3		
7	1	cup	tbs	16		

Present bad financial news in Roman numerals with ROMAN()

Want to obscure just how bad your numbers for the quarter are going to be? Use the =ROMAN() function to confuse everyone:

B1		f_x	=ROMAN(D1)	

	A	B	C	D	E
1		MCMXCIX	MM	1999	2000
2	Sales	CXLII	CXIV	142	114
3	COGS	XCIII	LXXXV	93	85
4	Gross Profit	XLIX	XXIX	49	29
5	Expenses	XXXV	XXVIII	35	28
6	Income	XIV	I	14	1

Compare errors in absolute terms with ABS()

You can find the Absolute Value of a number with =ABS(). This is good for measuring who had the largest error in their forecast.

D2		f_x	=ABS(C2-B2)	

	A	B	C	D	E
1	Rep	Forecast	Actual	Error	
2	Rep 4	195,000	95,000	100,000	
3	Rep 2	175,000	225,000	50,000	
4	Rep 1	125,000	115,000	10,000	
5	Rep 3	150,000	152,000	2,000	
6	Rep 5	123,490	123,490	0	

The absolute value of a negative number is the positive of that number. Absolute values are good for measuring scale of error.

Use random numbers to provide simulations with RAND()

The RAND() function generates a random number between 0 and 0.9999999 inclusive. This syntax is somewhat hard to remember.

If you multiply RAND() times 10, you get a range of numbers from 0 to 9.999999. Take the INT() of RAND()*10 and you have a nice random distribution of the digits from 0 to 9.

Since most people want to generate random numbers from 1 to something, it is common to add a 1 to the result.

This function simulates the roll of a six sided dice:

=INT(RAND()*6)+1

This function generates a random price between $25 and $44.99 rounded to 2 decimal places:

=25+ROUND(RAND()*20,2)

Get sales forecasts with =FORECAST()

If you have to generate the budget for next year, rather than pull a number out of a hat, let Excel predict it for you using the FORECAST() function.

	A	B	C	D	E
1	Year	Sales			
2	1	12000			
3	2	97000			
4	3	212000			
5	4	375000			
6					
7	Prediction:				
8	5	475000	=FORECAST(A8,B2:B5,A2:A5)		
9	6	595400			

Figure out the slope of a line with LINEST()

If you remember, any trend line is expressed as:

Y = mx+b

Where m is the slope and b is the y-intercept.

The TREND() and FORECAST() functions do this automatically, but every once in a while, you may want to know the m and b values that describe the trend line. LINEST is actually an array function, so you have to pluck the values out using INDEX.

	A	B	C	D	E	F
1	Year	Sales				
2	1	12000				
3	2	97000				
4	3	212000				
5	4	375000				
6						
7	slope	120400	=INDEX(LINEST($B$2:$B$5,$A$2:$A$5),1)			
8	Y-intercept	-127000	=INDEX(LINEST($B$2:$B$5,$A$2:$A$5),2)			
9						
10	Year	Prediction				
11	1	-6600	=$B$8+$B$7*A11			
12	2	113800	=$B$8+$B$7*A12			
13	3	234200	=$B$8+$B$7*A13			
14	4	354600	=$B$8+$B$7*A14			
15	5	475000	=$B$8+$B$7*A15			
16	6	595400	=$B$8+$B$7*A16			

In this example, B15:B16 duplicates the prediction shown by FORECAST(). However, we can also compare how well the forecasted trendline would have predicted the first four years. It does a pretty good job, so we might want to believe the FORECAST() results for this example.

Rewrite the CSE chapter with SUMPRODUCT()

To find the results of a SUMIF with two conditions, I suggested using CSE or array formulas. You can forget about trying to remember the Ctrl+Shift+Enter keystroke combination whe you use SUMPRODUCT()

	A	B	C	D	E	F	G
1	Region	Product	Sales				
2	East	Apples	14				
3	East	Bananas	16				
4	East	Apples	19				
5	East	Bananas	15				
6	Central	Apples	16				
7	Central	Bananas	10				
8	Central	Apples	15				
9	Central	Bananas	12				
10	West	Apples	14				
11	West	Bananas	16				
12	West	Apples	11				
13	West	Bananas	19				
14	West	Apples	13				
15							
16	Region:	Central	Central	West			
17	Product:	Bananas	Apples	Bananas			
18	Total:	22	31	35			
19	=SUMPRODUCT(($A$2:$A$14=B16)*($B$2:$B$14=B17)*($C$2:$C$14))						

Choose from a list with CHOOSE()

You really should use VLOOKUPs to do this, but if you have less than 29 choices, feel free to use CHOOSE.

	A	B	C	D	E	F
1	Selection	1				
2		Apple	=CHOOSE(B1,"Apple","Banana","Cherry")			

Test to see if a case is full with ISEVEN()

Do you pack items two to a case? Check to see if the case is full with =ISEVEN(A1).

Put 7th grade math teachers out of a job with GCD(), LCM(), FACT()

With all apologies to my 7th grade math teacher, Mr. Irwin, there really was no need to learn those horrible methods for calculating Greatest Common Denominator, Least Common Multiple, or Factorials.

Also, with apologies to my son Josh, because I waited until *after* he completed the whole sheet of problems before showing him this function to allow him to check his work.

	A	B	C	D
1	5474	28	14	=GCD(A1,B1)
2	9	6	18	=LCM(A2,B2)
3		6	720	=FACT(B3)

Impress your Lotus 1-2-3 friends with DAVERAGE()

Yes, most of the DFunctions were made totally obsolete with Pivot Tables, but they all still work. Anyone who was using Lotus 1-2-3 back in the '80s probably knows them. You can impress your boss by strutting out a DFunction once in a while.

	D	E	F	G	H	I
1	Product	Qty	Revenue		Product	
2	Premium Widget	8	952		Premium Widget	
3	Widget	45	4005			
4	Premium Widget	168	19992		Average Revenue for Premium Widgets	
5	Quality Widget	284	28116		26149.26727	
6	Premium Widget	60	7140		=DAVERAGE(A1:F1020,$F$1,H1:H2)	

There are many more cool functions!

The last few pages were a light-hearted sampling of what can be done with Excel functions. Peruse through the list of functions in the function reference once a while to see what can be done.

Appendix: Quick function reference

In case you ever forget whether the Interest or the Term comes first in the PMT() function, this quick reference will help to jog your memory. Listed here is every built-in function included in the basic Excel or in the Analysis Pack Add-In.

Arguments shown in Bold are required. Other arguments are optional. The functions are grouped by category. If you see something that looks interesting here, you can read more about that function in Excel help.

Functions marked with an asterisk (*) require the Analysis toolpack. Use Tools→Add-Ins to install this.

By the way, one last cool trick, in case you do forget the order of the arguments in a function:

➢ Start to type the function =PMT and then hit Ctrl+A.

The formula wizard appears to provide help with that function, reminding you of the order of the arguments.

Appendix table of contents

Database functions

Function	Type	Function	Type	Function	Type	Function	Type
ABS	Math	COLUMNS	Lookup	DOLLAR	Text & Data	GETPIVOTDATA	Database
ACCRINT	Financial	COMBIN	Math	DOLLARDE	Financial	GROWTH	Statistical
ACCRINTM	Financial	COMPLEX	Engineering	DOLLARFR	Financial	HARMEAN	Statistical
ACOS	Math	CONCATENATE	Text & Data	DPRODUCT	Database	HEX2BIN	Engineering
ACOSH	Math	CONFIDENCE	Statistical	DSTDEV	Database	HEX2DEC	Engineering
ADDRESS	Lookup	CONVERT	Engineering	DSTDEVP	Database	HEX2OCT	Engineering
AMORDEGRC	Financial	CORREL	Statistical	DSUM	Database	HLOOKUP	Lookup
AMORLINC	Financial	COS	Math	DURATION	Financial	HOUR	Date & Time
AND	Logical	COSH	Math	DVAR	Database	HYPERLINK	Lookup
AREAS	Lookup	COUNT	Statistical	DVARP	Database	HYPGEOMDIST	Statistical
ASC	Text & Data	COUNTA	Statistical	EDATE	Date & Time	IF	Logical
ASIN	Math	COUNTBLANK	Information	EFFECT	Financial	IMABS	Engineering
ASINH	Math	COUNTIF	Math	EOMONTH	Date & Time	IMAGINARY	Engineering
ATAN	Math	COUPDAYBS	Financial	ERF	Engineering	IMARGUMENT	Engineering
ATAN2	Math	COUPDAYS	Financial	ERFC	Engineering	IMCONJUGATE	Engineering
ATANH	Math	COUPDAYSNC	Financial	ERROR.TYPE	Information	IMCOS	Engineering
AVEDEV	Statistical	COUPNCD	Financial	EUROCONVERT	External	IMDIV	Engineering
AVERAGE	Statistical	COUPNUM	Financial	EVEN	Math	IMEXP	Engineering
AVERAGEA	Statistical	COUPPCD	Financial	EXACT	Text & Data	IMLN	Engineering
BAHTTEXT	Text	COVAR	Statistical	EXP	Math	IMLOG10	Engineering
BESSELI	Engineering	CRITBINOM	Statistical	EXPONDIST	Statistical	IMLOG2	Information
BESSELJ	Engineering	CUMIPMT	Financial	FACT	Math	IMPOWER	Information
BESSELK	Engineering	CUMPRINC	Financial	FACTDOUBLE	Math	IMPRODUCT	Information
BESSELY	Engineering	DATE	Date & Time	FALSE	Logical	IMREAL	Information
BETADIST	Statistical	DATEDIF	Date & Time	FDIST	Statistical	IMSIN	Information
BETAINV	Statistical	DATEVALUE	Date & Time	FIND	Text & Data	IMSQRT	Information
BIN2DEC	Engineering	DAVERAGE	Database	FINDB	Text & Data	IMSUB	Information
BIN2HEX	Engineering	DAY	Date & Time	FINV	Statistical	IMSUM	Information
BIN2OCT	Engineering	DAYS360	Date & Time	FISHER	Statistical	INDEX	Lookup
BINOMDIST	Statistical	DB	Financial	FISHERINV	Statistical	INDEX	Lookup
CALL	External	DCOUNT	Database	FIXED	Text & Data	INDIRECT	Lookup
CALL	External	DCOUNTA	Database	FLOOR	Math	INFO	Information
CALL	External	DDB	Financial	FORECAST	Statistical	INT	Math
CEILING	Math	DEC2BIN	Engineering	FREQUENCY	Statistical	INTERCEPT	Statistical
CELL	Information	DEC2HEX	Engineering	FTEST	Statistical	INTRATE	Financial
CHAR	Text & Data	DEC2OCT	Engineering	FV	Financial	IPMT	Financial
CHIDIST	Statistical	DEGREES	Math	FVSCHEDULE	Financial	IRR	Financial
CHIINV	Statistical	DELTA	Engineering	GAMMADIST	Statistical	ISBLANK	Information
CHITEST	Statistical	DEVSQ	Statistical	GAMMAINV	Statistical	ISERR	Information
CHOOSE	Lookup	DGET	Database	GAMMALN	Statistical	ISERROR	Information
CLEAN	Text & Data	DISC	Financial	GCD	Math	ISEVEN	Information
CODE	Text & Data	DMAX	Database	GEOMEAN	Statistical	ISLOGICAL	Information
COLUMN	Lookup	DMIN	Database	GESTEP	Engineering	ISNA	Information

Function	Type	Function	Type	Function	Type	Function	Type
ISNONTEXT	Information	NA	Information	RANK	Statistical	SUMX2MY2	Math
ISNUMBER	Information	NEGBINOMDIST	Statistical	RATE	Financial	SUMX2PY2	Math
ISODD	Financial	NETWORKDAYS	Date & Time	RECEIVED	Financial	SUMXMY2	Math
ISPMT	Financial	NOMINAL	Financial	REGISTER.ID	External	SYD	Financial
ISREF	Information	NORMDIST	Statistical	REGISTER.ID	External	T	Text & Data
ISTEXT	Information	NORMINV	Statistical	REPLACE	Text & Data	TAN	Math
JIS	Text & Data	NORMSDIST	Statistical	REPLACEB	Text & Data	TANH	Math
KURT	Statistical	NORMSINV	Statistical	REPT	Text & Data	TBILLEQ	Financial
LARGE	Statistical	NOT	Logical	RIGHT	Text & Data	TBILLPRICE	Financial
LCM	Math	NOW	Date & Time	RIGHTB	Text & Data	TBILLYIELD	Financial
LEFT	Text & Data	NPER	Financial	ROMAN	Math	TDIST	Statistical
LEFTB	Text & Data	NPV	Financial	ROUND	Math	TEXT	Text & Data
LEN	Text & Data	OCT2BIN	Information	ROUNDDOWN	Math	TIME	Date & Time
LENB	Text & Data	OCT2DEC	Information	ROUNDUP	Math	TIMEVALUE	Date & Time
LINEST	Statistical	OCT2HEX	Information	ROW	Lookup	TINV	Statistical
LN	Math	ODD	Math	ROWS	Lookup	TODAY	Date & Time
LOG	Math	ODDFPRICE	Financial	RSQ	Statistical	TRANSPOSE	Lookup
LOG10	Math	ODDFYIELD	Financial	RTD	Lookup	TREND	Statistical
LOGEST	Statistical	ODDLPRICE	Financial	SEARCH	Text & Data	TRIM	Text & Data
LOGINV	Statistical	ODDLYIELD	Financial	SEARCHB	Text & Data	TRUE	Logical
LOGNORMDIST	Statistical	OFFSET	Lookup	SECOND	Date & Time	TRUNC	Math
LOOKUP	Lookup	OR	Logical	SERIESSUM	Math	TTEST	Statistical
LOOKUP	Lookup	PEARSON	Statistical	SIGN	Math	TYPE	Information
LOWER	Text & Data	PERCENTILE	Statistical	SIN	Math	UPPER	Text & Data
MATCH	Lookup	PERCENTRANK	Statistical	SINH	Math	VALUE	Text & Data
MAX	Statistical	PERMUT	Statistical	SKEW	Statistical	VAR	Statistical
MAXA	Statistical	PHONETIC	Text & Data	SLN	Financial	VARA	Statistical
MDETERM	Math	PI	Math	SLOPE	Statistical	VARP	Statistical
MDURATION	Financial	PMT	Financial	SMALL	Statistical	VARPA	Statistical
MEDIAN	Statistical	POISSON	Statistical	SQL.REQUEST	External	VDB	Financial
MID	Text & Data	POWER	Math	SQRT	Math	VLOOKUP	Lookup
MIDB	Text & Data	PPMT	Financial	SQRTPI	Math	WEEKDAY	Date & Time
MIN	Statistical	PRICE	Financial	STANDARDIZE	Statistical	WEEKNUM	Date & Time
MINA	Statistical	PRICEDISC	Financial	STDEV	Statistical	WEIBULL	Statistical
MINUTE	Date & Time	PRICEMAT	Financial	STDEVA	Statistical	WORKDAY	Date & Time
MINVERSE	Math	PROB	Statistical	STDEVP	Statistical	XIRR	Financial
MIRR	Financial	PRODUCT	Math	STDEVPA	Statistical	XNPV	Financial
MMULT	Math	PROPER	Text & Data	STEYX	Statistical	YEAR	Date & Time
MOD	Math	PV	Financial	SUBSTITUTE	Text & Data	YEARFRAC	Date & Time
MODE	Statistical	QUARTILE	Statistical	SUBTOTAL	Math	YEN	Text & Data
MONTH	Date & Time	QUOTIENT	Math	SUM	Math	YIELD	Financial
MROUND	Math	RADIANS	Math	SUMIF	Math	YIELDDISC	Financial
MULTINOMIAL	Math	RAND	Math	SUMPRODUCT	Math	YIELDMAT	Financial
N	Information	RANDBETWEEN	Math	SUMSQ	Math	ZTEST	Statistical

Database functions

DAVERAGE(database,field,criteria)

Averages the values in a column in a list or database that match conditions that you specify. (See page 109)

DCOUNT(database,field,criteria)

Counts the cells that contain numbers in a column in a list or database that match conditions that you specify.

DCOUNTA(database,field,criteria)

Counts all of the nonblank cells in a column in a list or database that match conditions that you specify.

DGET(database,field,criteria)

Extracts a single value from a column in a list or database that matches conditions you specify.

DMAX(database,field,criteria)

Returns the largest number in a column in a list or database that matches conditions you specify.

DMIN(database,field,criteria)

Returns the smallest number in a column in a list or database that matches conditions you specify.

DPRODUCT(database,field,criteria)

Multiplies the values in a column in a list or database that match conditions that you specify.

DSTDEV(database,field,criteria)

Estimates the standard deviation of a population based on a sample, using the numbers in a column in a list or database that match conditions that you specify.

DSTDEVP(database,field,criteria)

Calculates the standard deviation of a population based on the entire population, using the numbers in a column in a list or database that match conditions that you specify.

DSUM(database,field,criteria)

Adds the numbers in a column in a list or database that match conditions that you specify.

DVAR(database,field,criteria)

Estimates the variance of a population based on a sample, using the numbers in a column in a list or database that match conditions that you specify.

DVARP(database,field,criteria)

Calculates the variance of a population based on the entire population, using the numbers in a column in a list or database that match conditions that you specify.

GETPIVOTDATA(pivot_table,name)

Returns data stored in a PivotTable report. You can use GETPIVOTDATA to retrieve summary data from a PivotTable report, provided the summary data is visible in the report.

Date and time functions

DATE(year,month,day)

Returns the serial number that represents a particular date. (See page 100)

DATEDIF(start_date,end_date,unit)

Calculates the number of days, months, or years between two dates. This function is provided for compatibility with Lotus 1-2-3.

DATEVALUE(date_text)

Returns the serial number of the date represented by date_text. Use DATEVALUE to convert a date represented by text to a serial number.

DAY(serial_number)

Returns the day of a date, represented by a serial number. The day is given as an integer ranging from 1 to 31. (See page 100)

DAYS360(start_date,end_date,method)

Returns the number of days between two dates based on a 360-day year (twelve 30-day months), which is used in some accounting calculations. Use this function to help compute payments if your accounting system is based on twelve 30-day months.

EDATE(start_date,months)*

Returns the serial number that represents the date that is the indicated number of months before or after a specified date (the start_date). Use EDATE to calculate maturity dates or due dates that fall on the same day of the month as the date of issue.

EOMONTH(start_date,months)*

Returns the serial number for the last day of the month that is the indicated number of months before or after start_date. Use EOMONTH to calculate maturity dates or due dates that fall on the last day of the month.

HOUR(serial_number)

Returns the hour of a time value. The hour is given as an integer, ranging from 0 (12:00 A.M.) to 23 (11:00 P.M.).

MINUTE(serial_number)

Returns the minutes of a time value. The minute is given as an integer, ranging from 0 to 59.

MONTH(serial_number)

Returns the month of a date represented by a serial number. The month is given as an integer, ranging from 1 (January) to 12 (December). (See page 100)

NETWORKDAYS(start_date,end_date,holidays)*

Returns the number of whole working days between start_date and end_date. Working days exclude weekends and any dates identified in holidays. Use NETWORKDAYS to calculate employee benefits that accrue based on the number of days worked during a specific term.

NOW( )

Returns the serial number of the current date and time. (See page 100)

SECOND(serial_number)

Returns the seconds of a time value. The second is given as an integer in the range 0 (zero) to 59.

TIME(hour,minute,second)

Returns the decimal number for a particular time. The decimal number returned by TIME is a value ranging from 0 to 0.99999999, representing the times from 0:00:00 (12:00:00 A.M.) to 23:59:59 (11:59:59 P.M.).

TIMEVALUE(time_text)

Returns the decimal number of the time represented by a text string. The decimal number is a value ranging from 0 (zero) to 0.99999999, representing the times from 0:00:00 (12:00:00 A.M.) to 23:59:59 (11:59:59 P.M.).

TODAY( )

Returns the serial number of the current date. The serial number is the date-time code used by Microsoft Excel for date and time calculations. (See pages 89 and 100)

WEEKDAY(serial_number,return_type)

Returns the day of the week corresponding to a date. The day is given as an integer, ranging from 1 (Sunday) to 7 (Saturday), by default.

WEEKNUM(serial_num,return_type)*

Returns a number that indicates where the week falls numerically within a year.

WORKDAY(start_date,days,holidays)*

Returns a number that represents a date that is the indicated number of working days before or after a date (the starting date). Working days exclude weekends and any dates identified as holidays. Use WORKDAY to exclude weekends or holidays when you calculate invoice due dates, expected delivery times, or the number of days of work performed. To view the number as a date, click Cells on the Format menu, click Date in the Category box, and then click a date format in the Type box.

YEAR(serial_number)

Returns the year corresponding to a date. The year is returned as an integer in the range 1900-9999. (See page 100)

YEARFRAC(start_date,end_date,basis)*

Calculates the fraction of the year represented by the number of whole days between two dates (the start_date and the end_date). Use the YEARFRAC worksheet function to identify the proportion of a whole year's benefits or obligations to assign to a specific term.

Engineering functions

BESSELI(x,n)*

Returns the modified Bessel function, which is equivalent to the Bessel function evaluated for purely imaginary arguments.

BESSELJ(x,n)*

Returns the Bessel function.

BESSELK(x,n)*

Returns the modified Bessel function, which is equivalent to the Bessel functions evaluated for purely imaginary arguments.

BESSELY(x,n)*

Returns the Bessel function, which is also called the Weber function or the Neumann function.

BIN2DEC(number)*

Converts a binary number to decimal.

BIN2HEX(number,places)*

Converts a binary number to hexadecimal.

BIN2OCT(number,places)*

Converts a binary number to octal.

COMPLEX(real_num,i_num,suffix)*

Converts real and imaginary coefficients into a complex number of the form $x + yi$ or $x + yj$.

CONVERT(number,from_unit,to_unit)*

Converts a number from one measurement system to another. For example, CONVERT can translate a table of distances in miles to a table of distances in kilometers. (See page 106)

DEC2BIN(number,places)*

Converts a decimal number to binary.

DEC2HEX(number,places)*

Converts a decimal number to hexadecimal.

DEC2OCT(number,places)*

Converts a decimal number to octal.

DELTA(number1,number2)*

Tests whether two values are equal. Returns 1 if number1 = number2; returns 0 otherwise. Use this function to filter a set of values. For example, by summing several DELTA functions you calculate the count of equal pairs. This function is also known as the Kronecker Delta function.

ERF(lower_limit,upper_limit)*

Returns the error function integrated between lower_limit and upper_limit.

ERFC(x)*

Returns the complementary ERF function integrated between x and infinity.

GESTEP(number,step)*

Returns 1 if number $\geq$ step; returns 0 (zero) otherwise. Use this function to filter a set of values. For example, by summing several GESTEP functions, you calculate the count of values that exceed a threshold.

HEX2BIN(number,places)*

Converts a hexadecimal number to binary.

HEX2DEC(number)*

Converts a hexadecimal number to decimal.

HEX2OCT(number,places)*

Converts a hexadecimal number to octal.

IMABS(inumber)*

Returns the absolute value (modulus) of a complex number in x + yi or x + yj text format.

IMAGINARY(inumber)*

Returns the imaginary coefficient of a complex number in x + yi or x + yj text format.

IMARGUMENT(inumber)*

Returns the argument θ (theta) an angle expressed in radians, such that:

$$x + yi = |x + yi| \times e^{i\theta} = |x + yi|(\cos\theta + i\sin\theta)$$

IMCONJUGATE(inumber)*

Returns the complex conjugate of a complex number in x + yi or x + yj text format.

IMCOS(inumber)*

Returns the cosine of a complex number in x + yi or x + yj text format.

IMDIV(inumber1,inumber2)*

Returns the quotient of two complex numbers in x + yi or x + yj text format.

IMEXP(inumber)*

Returns the exponential of a complex number in x + yi or x + yj text format.

IMLN(inumber)*

Returns the natural logarithm of a complex number in x + yi or x + yj text format.

IMLOG10(inumber)*

Returns the common logarithm (base 10) of a complex number in x + yi or x + yj text format.

IMLOG2(inumber)*

Returns the base-2 logarithm of a complex number in x + yi or x + yj text format.

IMPOWER(inumber,number)*

Returns a complex number in x + yi or x + yj text format raised to a power.

IMPRODUCT(inumber1,inumber2,...)*

Returns the product of 2 to 29 complex numbers in x + yi or x + yj text format.

IMREAL(inumber)*

Returns the real coefficient of a complex number in x + yi or x + yj text format.

IMSIN(inumber)*

Returns the sine of a complex number in x + yi or x + yj text format.

IMSQRT(inumber)*

Returns the square root of a complex number in x + yi or x + yj text format.

IMSUB(inumber1,inumber2)*

Returns the difference of two complex numbers in x + yi or x + yj text format.

IMSUM(inumber1,inumber2,...)*

Returns the sum of two or more complex numbers in x + yi or x + yj text format.

OCT2BIN(number,places)*

Converts an octal number to binary.

OCT2DEC(number)*

Converts an octal number to decimal.

OCT2HEX(number,places)

Converts an octal number to hexadecimal.

External functions

CALL(register_id,argument1,...)

Calls a procedure in a dynamic link library or code resource. Use this syntax only with a previously registered code resource, which uses arguments from the REGISTER function.

CALL(file_text,resource,type_text,argument1,...)

Calls a procedure in a dynamic link library or code resource. Use this syntax to simultaneously register and call a code resource for the Macintosh.

CALL(module_text,procedure,type_text,argument1,...)

Calls a procedure in a dynamic link library or code resource. Use this syntax to simultaneously register and call a code resource for Windows machines.

EUROCONVERT(number,source,target,full_precision,triangulation_precision)

New in Excel XP - Converts a number to euros, converts a number from euros to a euro member currency, or converts a number from one euro member currency to another by using the euro as an intermediary (triangulation). The currencies available for conversion are those of the European Union (EU) members that have adopted the euro.

REGISTER.ID(file_text,resource,type_text)

Returns the register ID of the specified dynamic link library (DLL) or code resource that has been previously registered. If the DLL or code resource has not been registered, this function registers the DLL or code resource and then returns the register ID for the Macintosh.

REGISTER.ID(module_text,procedure,type_text)

Returns the register ID of the specified dynamic link library (DLL) or code resource that has been previously registered. If the DLL or code resource has not been registered, this function registers the DLL or code resource and then returns the register ID for Windows.

SQL.REQUEST(connection_string,output_ref,driver_prompt,query_text,col_names_logical)*

Connects with an external data source, and runs a query from a worksheet. SQL.REQUEST then returns the result as an array without the need for macro programming. If this function is not already available, install the Microsoft Excel ODBC add-in (XLODBC.XLA).

Financial functions

ACCRINT(issue,first_interest,settlement,rate,par,frequency,basis)*

Returns the accrued interest for a security that pays periodic interest.

ACCRINTM(issue,maturity,rate,par,basis)*

Returns the accrued interest for a security that pays interest at maturity.

AMORDEGRC(cost,date_purchased,first_period,salvage,period,rate,basis)*

Returns the depreciation for each accounting period. This function is provide for the French accounting system. If an asset is purchased in the middle of the accounting period, the prorated depreciation is taken into account. The function is similar to AMORLINC, except that a depreciation coefficient is applied in the calculation depending on the life of the assets.

AMORLINC(cost,date_purchased,first_period,salvage,period,rate,basis)*

Returns the depreciation for each accounting period. This function is provided for the French accounting system. If an asset is purchased in the middle of the accounting period, the prorated depreciation is taken into account.

COUPDAYBS(settlement,maturity,frequency,basis)*

Returns the number of days from the beginning of the coupon period to the settlement date.

COUPDAYS(settlement,maturity,frequency,basis)*

Returns the number of days in the coupon period that contains the settlement date.

COUPDAYSNC(settlement,maturity,frequency,basis)*

Returns the number of days from the settlement date to the next coupon date.

COUPNCD(settlement,maturity,frequency,basis)*

Returns a number that represents the next coupon date after the settlement date. To view the number as a date, click Cells on the Format menu, click Date in the Category box, and then click a date format in the Type box.

COUPNUM(settlement,maturity,frequency,basis)*

Returns the number of coupons payable between the settlement date and maturity date, rounded up to the nearest whole coupon.

COUPPCD(settlement,maturity,frequency,basis)*

Returns a number that represents the previous coupon date before the settlement date. To view the number as a date, click Cells on the Format menu, click Date in the Category box, and then click a date format in the Type box.

CUMIPMT(rate,nper,pv,start_period,end_period,type)*

Returns the cumulative interest paid on a loan between start_period and end_period.

CUMPRINC(rate,nper,pv,start_period,end_period,type)*

Returns the cumulative principal paid on a loan between start_period and end_period.

DB(cost,salvage,life,period,month)

Returns the depreciation of an asset for a specified period using the fixed-declining balance method.

DDB(cost,salvage,life,period,factor)

Returns the depreciation of an asset for a specified period using the double-declining balance method or some other method you specify.

DISC(settlement,maturity,pr,redemption,basis)*

Returns the discount rate for a security.

DOLLARDE(fractional_dollar,fraction)*

Converts a dollar price expressed as a fraction into a dollar price expressed as a decimal number. Use DOLLARDE to convert fractional dollar numbers, such as securities prices, to decimal numbers.

DOLLARFR(decimal_dollar,fraction)*

Converts a dollar price expressed as a decimal number into a dollar price expressed as a fraction. Use DOLLARFR to convert decimal numbers to fractional dollar numbers, such as securities prices.

DURATION(settlement,maturity,coupon yld,frequency,basis)*

Returns the Macauley duration for an assumed par value of $100. Duration is defined as the weighted average of the present value of the cash flows and is used as a measure of a bond price's response to changes in yield.

EFFECT(nominal_rate,npery)*

Returns the effective annual interest rate, given the nominal annual interest rate and the number of compounding periods per year.

FV(rate,nper,pmt,pv,type)

Returns the future value of an investment based on periodic, constant payments and a constant interest rate.

FVSCHEDULE(principal,schedule)*

Returns the future value of an initial principal after applying a series of compound interest rates. Use FVSCHEDULE to calculate future value of an investment with a variable or adjustable rate.

INTRATE(settlement,maturity,investment,redemption,basis)*

Returns the interest rate for a fully invested security.

IPMT(rate,per,nper,pv,fv,type)

Returns the interest payment for a given period for an investment based on periodic, constant payments and a constant interest rate. For a more complete description of the arguments in IPMT and for more information about annuity functions, see PV.

IRR(values,guess)

Returns the internal rate of return for a series of cash flows represented by the numbers in values. These cash flows do not have to be even, as they would be for an annuity. However, the cash flows must occur at regular intervals, such as monthly or annually. The internal rate of return is the interest rate received for an investment consisting of payments (negative values) and income (positive values) that occur at regular periods.

ISPMT(rate,per,nper,pv)

Calculates the interest paid during a specific period of an investment. This function is provided for compatibility with Lotus 1-2-3.

MDURATION(settlement,maturity,coupon,yld,frequency,basis)*

Returns the modified duration for a security with an assumed par value of $100.

MIRR(values,finance_rate,reinvest_rate)

Returns the modified internal rate of return for a series of periodic cash flows. MIRR considers both the cost of the investment and the interest received on reinvestment of cash.

NOMINAL(effect_rate,npery)*

Returns the nominal annual interest rate, given the effective rate and the number of compounding periods per year.

NPER(rate, pmt, pv, fv, type)

Returns the number of periods for an investment based on periodic, constant payments and a constant interest rate.

NPV(rate,value1,value2, ...)

Calculates the net present value of an investment by using a discount rate and a series of future payments (negative values) and income (positive values).

ODDFPRICE(settlement,maturity,issue,first_coupon,rate,yld,redemption,frequency,basis)*

Returns the price per $100 face value of a security having an odd (short or long) first period.

ODDFYIELD(settlement,maturity,issue,first_coupon,rate,pr,redemption,frequency,basis)*

Returns the yield of a security that has an odd (short or long) first period.

ODDLPRICE(settlement,maturity,last_interest,rate,yld,redemption,frequency,basis)*

Returns the price per $100 face value of a security having an odd (short or long) last coupon period.

ODDLYIELD(settlement,maturity,last_interest,rate,pr,redemption,frequency,basis)*

Returns the yield of a security that has an odd (short or long) last period.

PMT(rate,nper,pv,fv,type)

Calculates the payment for a loan based on constant payments and a constant interest rate. (See page 105)

PPMT(rate,per,nper,pv,fv,type)

Returns the payment on the principal for a given period for an investment based on periodic, constant payments and a constant interest rate.

PRICE(settlement,maturity,rate,yld,redemption,frequency,basis)*

Returns the price per $100 face value of a security that pays periodic interest.

PRICEDISC(settlement,maturity,discount,redemption,basis)*

Returns the price per $100 face value of a discounted security.

PRICEMAT(settlement,maturity,issue,rate,yld,basis)*

Returns the price per $100 face value of a security that pays interest at maturity.

PV(rate,nper,pmt,fv,type)

Returns the present value of an investment. The present value is the total amount that a series of future payments is worth now. For example, when you borrow money, the loan amount is the present value to the lender.

RATE(nper,pmt,pv,fv,type,guess)

Returns the interest rate per period of an annuity. RATE is calculated by iteration and can have zero or more solutions. If the successive results of RATE do not converge to within 0.0000001 after 20 iterations, RATE returns the #NUM! error value.

RECEIVED(settlement,maturity,investment,discount,basis)*

Returns the amount received at maturity for a fully invested security.

SLN(cost,salvage,life)

Returns the straight-line depreciation of an asset for one period.

SYD(cost,salvage,life,per)

Returns the sum-of-years' digits depreciation of an asset for a specified period.

TBILLEQ(settlement,maturity,discount)*

Returns the bond-equivalent yield for a Treasury bill.

TBILLPRICE(settlement,maturity,discount)*

Returns the price per $100 face value for a Treasury bill.

TBILLYIELD(settlement,maturity,pr)*

Returns the yield for a Treasury bill.

VDB(cost,salvage,life,start_period,end_period,factor,no_switch)

Returns the depreciation of an asset for any period you specify, including partial periods, using the double-declining balance method or some other method you specify. VDB stands for variable declining balance.

XIRR(values,dates,guess)*

Returns the internal rate of return for a schedule of cash flows that is not necessarily periodic. To calculate the internal rate of return for a series of periodic cash flows, use the IRR function.

XNPV(rate,values,dates)*

Returns the net present value for a schedule of cash flows that is not necessarily periodic. To calculate the net present value for a series of cash flows that is periodic, use the NPV function.

YIELD(settlement,maturity,rate,pr,redemption,frequency,basis)*

Returns the yield on a security that pays periodic interest. Use YIELD to calculate bond yield.

YIELDDISC(settlement,maturity,pr,redemption,basis)*

Returns the annual yield for a discounted security.

YIELDMAT(settlement,maturity,issue,rate,pr,basis)*

Returns the annual yield of a security that pays interest at maturity.

Information functions

CELL(info_type,reference)

Returns information about the formatting, location, or contents of the upper-left cell in a reference. See page 90)

COUNTBLANK(range)

Counts empty cells in a specified range of cells.

ERROR.TYPE(error_val)*

Returns a number corresponding to one of the error values in Microsoft Excel or returns the #N/A error if no error exists. You can use ERROR.TYPE in an IF function to test for an error value and return a text string, such as a message, instead of the error value.

INFO(type_text)

Returns information about the current operating environment.

ISBLANK(value)

Returns TRUE if Value refers to an empty cell.

ISERROR(value)

Returns TRUE if Value refers to any error value (#N/A, #VALUE!, #REF!, #DIV/0!, #NUM!, #NAME?, or #NULL!).

ISERR(value)

Returns TRUE if Value refers to any error value except #N/A.

ISEVEN(number)*

Returns TRUE if number is even, or FALSE if number is odd. (See page 109)

ISLOGICAL(value)

Returns TRUE if Value refers to a logical value.

ISNA(value)

Returns TRUE if Value refers to the #N/A (value not available) error value. (See page 14)

ISNONTEXT(value)

Returns TRUE if Value refers to any item that is not text. (Note that this function returns TRUE if value refers to a blank cell.)

ISNUMBER(value)

Returns TRUE if Value refers to a number.

ISODD(number)*

Returns TRUE if number is odd, or FALSE if number is even.

ISREF(value)

Returns TRUE if Value refers to a reference.

ISTEXT(value)

Returns TRUE if Value refers to text.

N(value)

Returns a value converted to a number.

NA( )

Returns the error value #N/A. #N/A is the error value that means "no value is available." Use NA to mark empty cells. By entering #N/A in cells where you are missing information, you can avoid the problem of unintentionally including empty cells in your calculations. (When a formula refers to a cell containing #N/A, the formula returns the #N/A error value.)

TYPE(value)

Returns the type of value. Use TYPE when the behavior of another function depends on the type of value in a particular cell.

Logical functions

AND(logical1,logical2, ...)

Returns TRUE if all its arguments are TRUE; returns FALSE if one or more arguments is FALSE. (See page 98)

FALSE( )

Returns the logical value FALSE.

IF(logical_test,value_if_true,value_if_false)

Returns one value if a condition you specify evaluates to TRUE and another value if it evaluates to FALSE.

NOT(logical)

Reverses the value of its argument. Use NOT when you want to make sure a value is not equal to one particular value.

OR(logical1,logical2,...)

Returns TRUE if any argument is TRUE; returns FALSE if all arguments are FALSE.

TRUE( )

Returns the logical value TRUE.

Lookup functions

ADDRESS(row_num,column_num,abs_num,a1,sheet_text)

Creates a cell address as text, given specified row and column numbers.

AREAS(reference)

Returns the number of areas in a reference. An area is a range of contiguous cells or a single cell.

CHOOSE(index_num,value1,value2,...)

Uses index_num to return a value from the list of value arguments. Use CHOOSE to select one of up to 29 values based on the index number. For example, if value1 through value7 are the days of the week, CHOOSE returns one of the days when a number between 1 and 7 is used as index_num. (See page 109)

COLUMN(reference)

Returns the column number of the given reference.

COLUMNS(array)

Returns the number of columns in an array or reference.

HLOOKUP(lookup_value,table_array,row_index_num,range_lookup)

Searches for a value in the top row of a table or an array of values, and then returns a value in the same column from a row you specify in the table or array. Use HLOOKUP when your comparison values are located in a row across the top of a table of data, and you want to look down a specified number of rows. Use VLOOKUP when your comparison values are located in a column to the left of the data you want to find.

HYPERLINK(link_location,friendly_name)

Creates a shortcut or jump that opens a document stored on a network server, an intranet, or the Internet. When you click the cell that contains the HYPERLINK function, Microsoft Excel opens the file stored at link_location.

INDEX(array,row_num,column_num)

Returns the value of a specified cell or array of cells within array. (See pages 12 and 107)

INDEX(reference,row_num,column_num,area_num)

Returns a reference to a specified cell or cells within reference.

INDIRECT(ref_text,a1)

Returns the reference specified by a text string. References are immediately evaluated to display their contents. Use INDIRECT when you want to change the reference to a cell within a formula without changing the formula itself. (See page 89)

LOOKUP(lookup_value,lookup_vector,result_vector)

Returns a value either from a one-row or one-column range. This vector form of LOOKUP looks in a one-row or one-column range (known as a vector) for a value and returns a value from the same position in a second one-row or one-column range. Included for compatibility with other worksheets. Use VLOOKUP instead.

LOOKUP(lookup_value,array)

Returns a value from an array. The array form of LOOKUP looks in the first row or column of an array for the specified value and returns a value from the same position in the last row or column of the array. Included for compatibility with other spreadsheet programs. Use VLOOKUP instead.

MATCH(lookup_value,lookup_array,match_type)

Returns the relative position of an item in an array that matches a specified value in a specified order. Use MATCH instead of one of the LOOKUP functions when you need the position of an item in a range instead of the item itself. (See page 12)

OFFSET(reference,rows,cols,height,width)

Returns a reference to a range that is a specified number of rows and columns from a cell or range of cells. The reference that is returned can be a single cell or a range of cells. You can specify the number of rows and the number of columns to be returned. (See page 93)

ROW(reference)

Returns the row number of a reference.

ROWS(array)

Returns the number of rows in a reference or array.

RTD(ProgID,Server,Topic,[Topic2],...)

New in Excel XP – Retrieves real-time data from a program that supports COM automation.

TRANSPOSE(array)

Returns a vertical range of cells as a horizontal range, or vice versa. TRANSPOSE must be entered as an array formula in a range that has the same number of rows and columns, respectively, as array has columns and rows. Use TRANSPOSE to shift the vertical and horizontal orientation of an array on a worksheet. For example, some functions, such as LINEST, return horizontal arrays. LINEST returns a horizontal array of the slope and Y-intercept for a line.

VLOOKUP(lookup_value,table_array,col_index_num,range_lookup)

Searches for a value in the leftmost column of a table, and then returns a value in the same row from a column you specify in the table. Use VLOOKUP instead of HLOOKUP when your comparison values are located in a column to the left of the data you want to find. (See page 9)

Math functions

ABS(number)

Returns the absolute value of a number. The absolute value of a number is the number without its sign. (See page 106)

ACOS(number)

Returns the arccosine of a number. The arccosine is the angle whose cosine is number. The returned angle is given in radians in the range 0 (zero) to pi.

ACOSH(number)

Returns the inverse hyperbolic cosine of a number. Number must be greater than or equal to 1. The inverse hyperbolic cosine is the value whose hyperbolic cosine is number, so ACOSH(COSH(number)) equals number.

ASIN(number)

Returns the arcsine of a number. The arcsine is the angle whose sine is number. The returned angle is given in radians in the range -pi/2 to pi/2.

ASINH(number)

Returns the inverse hyperbolic sine of a number. The inverse hyperbolic sine is the value whose hyperbolic sine is number, so ASINH(SINH(number)) equals number.

ATAN(number)

Returns the arctangent of a number. The arctangent is the angle whose tangent is number. The returned angle is given in radians in the range -pi/2 to pi/2.

ATAN2(x_num,y_num)

Returns the arctangent of the specified x- and y-coordinates. The arctangent is the angle from the x-axis to a line containing the origin (0, 0) and a point with coordinates (x_num, y_num). The angle is given in radians between -pi and pi, excluding -pi.

ATANH(number)

Returns the inverse hyperbolic tangent of a number. Number must be between -1 and 1 (excluding -1 and 1). The inverse hyperbolic tangent is the value whose hyperbolic tangent is number, so ATANH(TANH(number)) equals number.

CEILING(number,significance)

Returns number rounded up, away from zero, to the nearest multiple of significance. For example, if you want to avoid using pennies in your prices and your product is priced at $4.42, use the formula =CEILING(4.42,0.05) to round prices up to the nearest nickel. (See page 105)

COMBIN(number,number_chosen)

Returns the number of combinations for a given number of items. Use COMBIN to determine the total possible number of groups for a given number of items.

COS(number)

Returns the cosine of the given angle.

COSH(number)

Returns the hyperbolic cosine of a number.

COUNTIF(range,criteria)

Counts the number of cells within a range that meet the given criteria. (See pages 58 and 102)

DEGREES(angle)

Converts radians into degrees.

EVEN(number)

Returns number rounded up to the nearest even integer. You can use this function for processing items that come in twos. For example, a packing crate accepts rows of one or two items. The crate is full when the number of items, rounded up to the nearest two, matches the crate's capacity.

EXP(number)

Returns e raised to the power of number. The constant e equals 2.71828182845904, the base of the natural logarithm.

FACT(number)

Returns the factorial of a number. The factorial of a number is equal to 1*2*3*...* number. (See page 109)

FACTDOUBLE(number)*

Returns the double factorial of a number.

FLOOR(number,significance)

Rounds number down, toward zero, to the nearest multiple of significance.

GCD(number1,number2, ...)*

Returns the greatest common divisor of two or more integers. The greatest common divisor is the largest integer that divides both number1 and number2 without a remainder. (See page 109)

INT(number)

Rounds a number down to the nearest integer. (See page 107)

LCM(number1,number2, ...)*

Returns the least common multiple of integers. The least common multiple is the smallest positive integer that is a multiple of all integer arguments number1, number2, and so on. Use LCM to add fractions with different denominators. (See page 109)

LN(number)

Returns the natural logarithm of a number. Natural logarithms are based on the constant e (2.71828182845904).

LOG(number,base)

Returns the logarithm of a number to the base you specify.

LOG10(number)

Returns the base-10 logarithm of a number.

MDETERM(array)

Returns the matrix determinant of an array.

MINVERSE(array)

Returns the inverse matrix for the matrix stored in an array.

MMULT(array1,array2)

Returns the matrix product of two arrays. The result is an array with the same number of rows as array1 and the same number of columns as array2.

MOD(number,divisor)

Returns the remainder after number is divided by divisor. The result has the same sign as divisor.

MROUND(number,multiple)*

Returns a number rounded to the desired multiple.

MULTINOMIAL(number1,number2, ...)*

Returns the ratio of the factorial of a sum of values to the product of factorials.

ODD(number)

Returns number rounded up to the nearest odd integer.

PI( )

Returns the number 3.14159265358979, the mathematical constant pi, accurate to 15 digits.

POWER(number,power)

Returns the result of a number raised to a power.

PRODUCT(number1,number2, ...)

Multiplies all the numbers given as arguments and returns the product.

QUOTIENT(numerator,denominator)*

Returns the integer portion of a division. Use this function when you want to discard the remainder of a division.

RADIANS(angle)

Converts degrees to radians.

RAND( )

Returns an evenly distributed random number greater than or equal to 0 and less than 1. A new random number is returned every time the worksheet is calculated. (See page 107)

RANDBETWEEN(bottom,top)*

Returns a random number between the numbers you specify. A new random number is returned every time the worksheet is calculated.

ROMAN(number,form)

Converts an arabic numeral to roman, as text. (See page 106)

ROUND(number,num_digits)

Rounds a number to a specified number of digits. (See page 107)

ROUNDDOWN(number,num_digits)

Rounds a number down, toward zero.

ROUNDUP(number,num_digits)

Rounds a number up, away from 0 (zero).

SERIESSUM(x,n,m,coefficients)*

Returns the sum of a power series based on the formula:

$$SERIES(x,n,m,a) \approx a_1x^n + a_2x^{(n+m)} + a_3x^{(n+2m)} + ... + a_ix^{(n+(i-1)m)}$$

SIGN(number)

Determines the sign of a number. Returns 1 if the number is positive, zero (0) if the number is 0, and -1 if the number is negative.

SIN(number)

Returns the sine of the given angle.

SINH(number)

Returns the hyperbolic sine of a number.

SQRT(number)

Returns a positive square root.

SQRTPI(number)*

Returns the square root of (number * pi).

SUBTOTAL(function_num,ref1,ref2,...)

Returns a subtotal in a list or database. It is generally easier to create a list with subtotals using the Subtotals command (Data menu). Once the subtotal list is created, you can modify it by editing the SUBTOTAL function.

SUM(number1,number2, ...)

Adds all the numbers in a range of cells. (See pages 59, 93, and 97)

SUMIF(range,criteria,sum_range)

Adds the cells specified by a given criteria. (See page 57)

SUMPRODUCT(array1,array2,array3, ...)

Multiplies corresponding components in the given arrays, and returns the sum of those products. (See page 108)

SUMSQ(number1,number2, ...)

Returns the sum of the squares of the arguments.

SUMX2MY2(array_x,array_y)

Returns the sum of the difference of squares of corresponding values in two arrays.

SUMX2PY2(array_x,array_y)

Returns the sum of the sum of squares of corresponding values in two arrays. The sum of the sum of squares is a common term in many statistical calculations.

SUMXMY2(array_x,array_y)

Returns the sum of squares of differences of corresponding values in two arrays.

TAN(number)

Returns the tangent of the given angle.

TANH(number)

Returns the hyperbolic tangent of a number.

TRUNC(number,num_digits)

Truncates a number to an integer by removing the fractional part of the number.

Statistical functions

AVEDEV(number1,number2, ...)

Returns the average of the absolute deviations of data points from their mean. AVEDEV is a measure of the variability in a data set.

AVERAGE(number1,number2, ...)

Returns the average (arithmetic mean) of the arguments. (See pages 52 and 62)

AVERAGEA(value1,value2,...)

Calculates the average (arithmetic mean) of the values in the list of arguments. In addition to numbers, text and logical values such as TRUE and FALSE are included in the calculation.

BETADIST(x,alpha,beta,A,B)

Returns the cumulative beta probability density function. The cumulative beta probability density function is commonly used to study variation in the percentage of something across samples, such as the fraction of the day people spend watching television.

BETAINV(probability,alpha,beta,A,B)

Returns the inverse of the cumulative beta probability density function. That is, if probability = BETADIST(x,...), then BETAINV(probability,...) = x. The cumulative beta distribution can be used in project planning to model probable completion times given an expected completion time and variability.

BINOMDIST(number_s,trials,probability_s,cumulative)

Returns the individual term binomial distribution probability. Use BINOMDIST in problems with a fixed number of tests or trials, when the outcomes of any trial are only success or failure, when trials are independent, and when the probability of success is constant throughout the experiment. For example, BINOMDIST can calculate the probability that two of the next three babies born are male.

CHIDIST(x,degrees_freedom)

Returns the one-tailed probability of the chi-squared distribution. The $\gamma2$ distribution is associated with a $\gamma2$ test. Use the $\gamma2$ test to compare observed and expected values. For example, a genetic experiment might hypothesize that the next generation of plants will exhibit a certain set of colors. By comparing the observed results with the expected ones, you can decide whether your original hypothesis is valid.

CHIINV(probability,degrees_freedom)

Returns the inverse of the one-tailed probability of the chi-squared distribution. If probability = CHIDIST(x,...), then CHIINV(probability,...) = x. Use this function to compare observed results with expected ones to decide whether your original hypothesis is valid.

CHITEST(actual_range,expected_range)

Returns the test for independence. CHITEST returns the value from the chi-squared ($\gamma2$) distribution for the statistic and the appropriate degrees of freedom. You can use $\gamma2$ tests to determine whether hypothesized results are verified by an experiment.

CONFIDENCE(alpha,standard_dev,size)

Returns the confidence interval for a population mean. The confidence interval is a range on either side of a sample mean. For example, if you order a product through the mail, you can determine, with a particular level of confidence, the earliest and latest the product will arrive.

CORREL(array1,array2)

Returns the correlation coefficient of the array1 and array2 cell ranges. Use the correlation coefficient to determine the relationship between two properties. For example, you can examine the relationship between a location's average temperature and the use of air conditioners.

COUNT(value1,value2, ...)

Counts the number of cells that contain numbers and numbers within the list of arguments. Use COUNT to get the number of entries in a number field in a range or array of numbers.

COUNTA(value1,value2, ...)

Counts the number of cells that are not empty and the values within the list of arguments. Use COUNTA to count the number of cells that contain data in a range or array.

COVAR(array1,array2)

Returns covariance, the average of the products of deviations for each data point pair. Use covariance to determine the relationship between two data sets. For example, you can examine whether greater income accompanies greater levels of education.

CRITBINOM(trials,probability_s,alpha)

Returns the smallest value for which the cumulative binomial distribution is greater than or equal to a criterion value. Use this function for quality assurance applications. For example, use CRITBINOM to determine the greatest number of defective parts that are allowed to come off an assembly line run without rejecting the entire lot.

DEVSQ(number1,number2,...)

Returns the sum of squares of deviations of data points from their sample mean.

EXPONDIST(x,lambda,cumulative)

Returns the exponential distribution. Use EXPONDIST to model the time between events, such as how long an automated bank teller takes to deliver cash. For example, you can use EXPONDIST to determine the probability that the process takes at most 1 minute.

FDIST(x,degrees_freedom1,degrees_freedom2)

Returns the F probability distribution. You can use this function to determine whether two data sets have different degrees of diversity. For example, you can examine test scores given to men and women entering high school and determine if the variability in the females is different from that found in the males.

FINV(probability,degrees_freedom1,degrees_freedom2)

Returns the inverse of the F probability distribution. If p = FDIST(x,...), then FINV(p,...) = x.

FISHER(x)

Returns the Fisher transformation at x. This transformation produces a function that is approximately normally distributed rather than skewed. Use this function to perform hypothesis testing on the correlation coefficient.

FISHERINV(y)

Returns the inverse of the Fisher transformation. Use this transformation when analyzing correlations between ranges or arrays of data. If y = FISHER(x), then FISHERINV(y) = x.

FORECAST(x,known_y's,known_x's)

Calculates, or predicts, a future value by using existing values. The predicted value is a y-value for a given x-value. The known values are existing x-values and y-values, and the new value is predicted by using linear regression. You can use this function to predict future sales, inventory requirements, or consumer trends. (See page 107)

FREQUENCY(data_array,bins_array)

Calculates how often values occur within a range of values, and then returns a vertical array of numbers. For example, use FREQUENCY to count the number of test scores that fall within ranges of scores. Because FREQUENCY returns an array, it must be entered as an array formula.

FTEST(array1,array2)

Returns the result of an F-test. An F-test returns the one-tailed probability that the variances in array1 and array2 are not significantly different. Use this function to determine whether two samples have different variances. For example, given test scores from public and private schools, you can test whether these schools have different levels of diversity.

GAMMADIST(x,alpha,beta,cumulative)

Returns the gamma distribution. You can use this function to study variables that may have a skewed distribution. The gamma distribution is commonly used in queuing analysis.

GAMMAINV(probability,alpha,beta)

Returns the inverse of the gamma cumulative distribution. If p = GAMMADIST(x,...), then GAMMAINV(p,...) = x.

GAMMALN(x)

Returns the natural logarithm of the gamma function, $\Gamma(x)$.

GEOMEAN(number1,number2, ...)

Returns the geometric mean of an array or range of positive data. For example, you can use GEOMEAN to calculate average growth rate given compound interest with variable rates.

GROWTH(known_y's,known_x's,new_x's,const)

Calculates predicted exponential growth by using existing data. GROWTH returns the y-values for a series of new x-values that you specify by using existing x-values and y-values. You can also use the GROWTH worksheet function to fit an exponential curve to existing x-values and y-values.

HARMEAN(number1,number2, ...)

Returns the harmonic mean of a data set. The harmonic mean is the reciprocal of the arithmetic mean of reciprocals.

HYPGEOMDIST(sample_s,number_sample,population_s,number_population)

Returns the hypergeometric distribution. HYPGEOMDIST returns the probability of a given number of sample successes, given the sample size, population successes, and population size. Use HYPGEOMDIST for problems with a finite population, where each observation is either a success or a failure, and where each subset of a given size is chosen with equal likelihood.

INTERCEPT(known_y's,known_x's)

Calculates the point at which a line will intersect the y-axis by using existing x-values and y-values. The intercept point is based on a best-fit regression line plotted through the known x-values and known y-values. Use the intercept when you want to determine the value of the dependent variable when the independent variable is 0 (zero). For example, you can use the INTERCEPT function to predict a metal's electrical resistance at 0°C when your data points were taken at room temperature and higher.

KURT(number1,number2, ...)

Returns the kurtosis of a data set. Kurtosis characterizes the relative peakedness or flatness of a distribution compared with the normal distribution. Positive kurtosis indicates a relatively peaked distribution. Negative kurtosis indicates a relatively flat distribution.

LARGE(array,k)

Returns the k-th largest value in a data set. You can use this function to select a value based on its relative standing. For example, you can use LARGE to return the highest, runner-up, or third-place score.

LINEST(known_y's,known_x's,const,stats)

Calculates the statistics for a line by using the "least squares" method to calculate a straight line that best fits your data, and returns an array that describes the line. Because this function returns an array of values, it must be entered as an array formula. (See page 107)

LOGEST(known_y's,known_x's,const,stats)

In regression analysis, calculates an exponential curve that fits your data and returns an array of values that describes the curve. Because this function returns an array of values, it must be entered as an array formula.

LOGINV(probability,mean,standard_dev)

Returns the inverse of the lognormal cumulative distribution function of x, where ln(x) is normally distributed with parameters mean and standard_dev. If p = LOGNORMDIST(x,...) then LOGINV(p,...) = x.

LOGNORMDIST(x,mean,standard_dev)

Returns the cumulative lognormal distribution of x, where ln(x) is normally distributed with parameters mean and standard_dev. Use this function to analyze data that has been logarithmically transformed.

MAX(number1,number2,...)

Returns the largest value in a set of values. (See pages 23 and 26)

MAXA(value1,value2,...)

Returns the largest value in a list of arguments. Text and logical values such as TRUE and FALSE are compared as well as numbers.

MEDIAN(number1,number2, ...)

Returns the median of the given numbers. The median is the number in the middle of a set of numbers; that is, half the numbers have values that are greater than the median, and half have values that are less.

MIN(number1,number2, ...)

Returns the smallest number in a set of values. (See page 26)

MINA(value1,value2,...)

Returns the smallest value in the list of arguments. Text and logical values such as TRUE and FALSE are compared as well as numbers.

MODE(number1,number2, ...)

Returns the most frequently occurring, or repetitive, value in an array or range of data. Like MEDIAN, MODE is a location measure.

NEGBINOMDIST(number_f,number_s,probability_s)

Returns the negative binomial distribution. NEGBINOMDIST returns the probability that there will be number_f failures before the number_s-th success, when the constant probability of a success is probability_s. This function is similar to the binomial distribution, except that the number of successes is fixed, and the number of trials is variable. Like the binomial, trials are assumed to be independent.

NORMDIST(x,mean,standard_dev,cumulative)

Returns the normal cumulative distribution for the specified mean and standard deviation. This function has a very wide range of applications in statistics, including hypothesis testing.

NORMINV(probability,mean,standard_dev)

Returns the inverse of the normal cumulative distribution for the specified mean and standard deviation.

NORMSDIST(z)

Returns the standard normal cumulative distribution function. The distribution has a mean of 0 (zero) and a standard deviation of one. Use this function in place of a table of standard normal curve areas.

NORMSINV(probability)

Returns the inverse of the standard normal cumulative distribution. The distribution has a mean of zero and a standard deviation of one.

PEARSON(array1,array2)

Returns the Pearson product moment correlation coefficient, r, a dimensionless index that ranges from -1.0 to 1.0 inclusive and reflects the extent of a linear relationship between two data sets.

PERCENTILE(array,k)

Returns the k-th percentile of values in a range. You can use this function to establish a threshold of acceptance. For example, you can decide to examine candidates who score above the 90th percentile.

PERCENTRANK(array,x,significance)

Returns the rank of a value in a data set as a percentage of the data set. This function can be used to evaluate the relative standing of a value within a data set. For example, you can use PERCENTRANK to evaluate the standing of an aptitude test score among all scores for the test.

PERMUT(number,number_chosen)

Returns the number of permutations for a given number of objects that can be selected from number objects. A permutation is any set or subset of objects or events where internal order is significant. Permutations are different from combinations, for which the internal order is not significant. Use this function for lottery-style probability calculations.

POISSON(x,mean,cumulative)

Returns the Poisson distribution. A common application of the Poisson distribution is predicting the number of events over a specific time, such as the number of cars arriving at a toll plaza in 1 minute.

PROB(x_range,prob_range,lower_limit,upper_limit)

Returns the probability that values in a range are between two limits. If upper_limit is not supplied, returns the probability that values in x_range are equal to lower_limit.

QUARTILE(array,quart)

Returns the quartile of a data set. Quartiles often are used in sales and survey data to divide populations into groups. For example, you can use QUARTILE to find the top 25 percent of incomes in a population.

RANK(number,ref,order)

Returns the rank of a number in a list of numbers. The rank of a number is its size relative to other values in a list. (If you were to sort the list, the rank of the number would be its position.) (See page 102)

RSQ(known_y's,known_x's)

Returns the square of the Pearson product moment correlation coefficient through data points in known_y's and known_x's. The r-squared value can be interpreted as the proportion of the variance in y attributable to the variance in x.

SKEW(number1,number2,...)

Returns the skewness of a distribution. Skewness characterizes the degree of asymmetry of a distribution around its mean. Positive skewness indicates a distribution with an asymmetric tail extending toward more positive values. Negative skewness indicates a distribution with an asymmetric tail extending toward more negative values.

SLOPE(known_y's,known_x's)

Returns the slope of the linear regression line through data points in known_y's and known_x's. The slope is the vertical distance divided by the horizontal distance between any two points on the line, which is the rate of change along the regression line.

SMALL(array,k)

Returns the k-th smallest value in a data set. Use this function to return values with a particular relative standing in a data set.

STANDARDIZE(x,mean,standard_dev)

Returns a normalized value from a distribution characterized by mean and standard_dev.

STDEV(number1,number2,...)

Estimates standard deviation based on a sample. The standard deviation is a measure of how widely values are dispersed from the average value (the mean).

STDEVA(value1,value2,...)

Estimates standard deviation based on a sample. The standard deviation is a measure of how widely values are dispersed from the average value (the mean). Text and logical values such as TRUE and FALSE are included in the calculation.

STDEVP(number1,number2,...)

Calculates standard deviation based on the entire population given as arguments. The standard deviation is a measure of how widely values are dispersed from the average value (the mean).

STDEVPA(value1,value2,...)

Calculates standard deviation based on the entire population given as arguments, including text and logical values. The standard deviation is a measure of how widely values are dispersed from the average value (the mean).

STEYX(known_y's,known_x's)

Returns the standard error of the predicted y-value for each x in the regression. The standard error is a measure of the amount of error in the prediction of y for an individual x.

TDIST(x,degrees_freedom,tails)

Returns the Percentage Points (probability) for the Student t-distribution where a numeric value (x) is a calculated value of t for which the Percentage Points are to be computed. The t-distribution is used in the hypothesis testing of small sample data sets. Use this function in place of a table of critical values for the t-distribution.

TINV(probability,degrees_freedom)

Returns the t-value of the Student's t-distribution as a function of the probability and the degrees of freedom.

TREND(known_y's,known_x's,new_x's,const)

Returns values along a linear trend. Fits a straight line (using the method of least squares) to the arrays known_y's and known_x's. Returns the y-values along that line for the array of new_x's that you specify. (See page 107)

TRIMMEAN(array,percent)

Returns the mean of the interior of a data set. TRIMMEAN calculates the mean taken by excluding a percentage of data points from the top and bottom tails of a data set. You can use this function when you wish to exclude outlying data from your analysis.

TTEST(array1,array2,tails,type)

Returns the probability associated with a Student's t-Test. Use TTEST to determine whether two samples are likely to have come from the same two underlying populations that have the same mean.

VAR(number1,number2,...)

Estimates variance based on a sample.

VARA(value1,value2,...)

Estimates variance based on a sample. In addition to numbers, text and logical values such as TRUE and FALSE are included in the calculation.

VARP(number1,number2,...)

Calculates variance based on the entire population.

VARPA(value1,value2,...)

Calculates variance based on the entire population. In addition to numbers, text and logical values such as TRUE and FALSE are included in the calculation.

WEIBULL(x,alpha,beta,cumulative)

Returns the Weibull distribution. Use this distribution in reliability analysis, such as calculating a device's mean time to failure.

ZTEST(array,x,sigma)

Returns the two-tailed P-value of a z-test. The z-test generates a standard score for x with respect to the data set, array, and returns the two-tailed probability for the normal distribution. You can use this function to assess the likelihood that a particular observation is drawn from a particular population.

Text and data functions

ASC(text)

Changes full-width (double-byte) English letters or katakana within a character string to half-width (single-byte) characters.

BAHTTEXT(number)

New in Excel XP: Converts a number to Thai text and adds a suffix of "Baht".

CHAR(number)

Returns the character specified by a number. Use CHAR to translate code page numbers you might get from files on other types of computers into characters.

CLEAN(text)

Removes all nonprintable characters from text. Use CLEAN on text imported from other applications that contains characters that may not print with your operating system. For example, you can use CLEAN to remove some low-level computer code that is frequently at the beginning and end of data files and cannot be printed.

CODE(text)

Returns a numeric code for the first character in a text string. The returned code corresponds to the character set used by your computer.

CONCATENATE(text1,text2,...)

Joins several text strings into one text string.

DOLLAR(number,decimals)

Converts a number to text using currency format, with the decimals rounded to the specified place. The format used is $#,##0.00_);($#,##0.00).

EXACT(text1,text2)

Compares two text strings and returns TRUE if they are exactly the same, FALSE otherwise. EXACT is case-sensitive but ignores formatting differences. Use EXACT to test text being entered into a document.

FIND(find_text,within_text,start_num)

FIND finds one text string (find_text) within another text string (within_text), and returns the number of the starting position of find_text, from the first character of within_text. You can also use SEARCH to find one text string within another, but unlike SEARCH, FIND is case sensitive and doesn't allow wildcard characters. (See page 99)

FINDB(find_text,within_text,start_num)

FINDB finds one text string (find_text) within another text string (within_text), and returns the number of the starting position of find_text, based on the number of bytes each character uses, from the first character of within_text. This function is for use with double-byte characters. You can also use SEARCHB to find one text string within another.

FIXED(number,decimals,no_commas)

Rounds a number to the specified number of decimals, formats the number in decimal format using a period and commas, and returns the result as text.

JIS(text)

Changes half-width (single-byte) English letters or katakana within a character string to full-width (double-byte) characters.

LEFT(text,num_chars)

LEFT returns the first character or characters in a text string, based on the number of characters you specify. (See page 99)

LEFTB(text,num_bytes)

LEFTB returns the first character or characters in a text string, based on the number of bytes you specify. This function is for use with double-byte characters.

LEN(text)

LEN returns the number of characters in a text string. (See pages 62 and 99)

LENB(text)

LENB returns the number of bytes used to represent the characters in a text string. This function is for use with double-byte characters.

LOWER(text)

Converts all uppercase letters in a text string to lowercase. (See page 99)

MID(text,start_num,num_chars)

MID returns a specific number of characters from a text string, starting at the position you specify, based on the number of characters you specify. (See page 99)

MIDB(text,start_num,num_bytes)

MIDB returns a specific number of characters from a text string, starting at the position you specify, based on the number of bytes you specify. This function is for use with double-byte characters.

PHONETIC(reference)

Extracts the phonetic (furigana) characters from a text string.

PROPER(text)

Capitalizes the first letter in a text string and any other letters in text that follow any character other than a letter. Converts all other letters to lowercase letters. (See page 99)

REPLACE(old_text,start_num,num_chars,new_text)

REPLACE replaces part of a text string, based on the number of characters you specify, with a different text string.

REPLACEB(old_text,start_num,num_bytes,new_text)

REPLACEB replaces part of a text string, based on the number of bytes you specify, with a different text string. This function is for use with double-byte characters.

REPT(text,number_times)

Repeats text a given number of times. Use REPT to fill a cell with a number of instances of a text string.

RIGHT(text,num_chars)

RIGHT returns the last character or characters in a text string, based on the number of characters you specify. (See page 99)

RIGHTB(text,num_bytes)

RIGHTB returns the last character or characters in a text string, based on the number of bytes you specify. This function is for use with double-byte characters.

SEARCH(find_text,within_text,start_num)

SEARCH returns the number of the character at which a specific character or text string is first found, beginning with start_num. Use SEARCH to determine the location of a character or text string within another text string so that you can use the MID or REPLACE functions to change the text.

SEARCHB(find_text,within_text,start_num)

SEARCHB also finds one text string (find_text) within another text string (within_text), and returns the number of the starting position of find_text. The result is based on the number of bytes each character uses, beginning with start_num. This function is for use with double-byte characters You can also use FINDB to find one text string within another.

SUBSTITUTE(text,old_text,new_text,instance_num)

Substitutes new_text for old_text in a text string. Use SUBSTITUTE when you want to replace specific text in a text string; use REPLACE when you want to replace any text that occurs in a specific location in a text string.

T(value)

Returns the text referred to by value.

TEXT(value,format_text)

Converts a value to text in a specific number format. (See page 89)

TRIM(text)

Removes all spaces from text except for single spaces between words. Use TRIM on text that you have received from another application that may have irregular spacing. (See page 99)

UPPER(text)

Converts text to uppercase. (See page 99)

VALUE(text)

Converts a text string that represents a number to a number.

YEN(number,decimals)

Converts a number to text, using the ¥ (yen) currency format, with the number rounded to a specified place.

Afterword

Veni, vidi, vici

You came, you saw, you conquered. Congratulations!

There are a lot of amazing techniques in Guerilla Analysis Using Microsoft Excel. It is cool stuff that empowers you to run circles around your co-workers. I want you to be aware that there is something even better. Every copy of Microsoft Excel shipped in the last eight years includes an amazing tool. It is installed by default. You have it on your desktop right now. It is there, hiding behind your spreadsheet and most people don't even know it is there. It is Visual Basic for Applications–also known as VBA. This is the same Visual Basic language that you can buy from Microsoft for $936, except it is totally geared toward the Office product. Every single technique that I discussed in this book can be automated using VBA. Read the sidebar for an example that you can relate to:

A certain company spent $16 million installing an Oracle system. The standard Oracle reports didn't provide the information that this company needed to run the business. A lady named Valerie figured out how to pull data from Oracle, import it to Excel, then about five pivot tables later, she had a report for her department. She handed this to her manager, and Valerie was crowned the hero of the day. She whistled a bit as she floated back to her desk. Can you predict what the manager did? He showed it to another department manager down the hall. The other manager thought it was great and asked if Val could produce that same report for his department. She did. The next day, these two managers, Frick and Frack, walked into the big company meeting to show off their hot reports. They were all the rage.

There were 48 departments in that company, and the next month Valerie found herself doing 48 reports, one for every department. Her job now included doing these MONTHLY. She was fast, and could do each report in about 50 minutes, but she still found herself spending 40 hours each month manually producing these reports. Then, Valerie happened to find my web site. Every single action that you do in Excel or Office can be automated. These were tough reports. The company had exceptions that Oracle did not capture. Val had knowledge that certain cost centers had to be excluded or reclassed. Certain pivot tables had to include a reversal of certain accounts. It was about as bizarre a report as you could possibly explain. (I understand why the high-priced Oracle consultants with their Discoverer tools couldn't figure out how to express the report in a single SQL statement.) Before the next month rolled around, Valerie had a custom VBA application from MrExcel. The 40-hour ordeal was replaced with two button clicks and about 4 minutes of time.

MrExcel.com consulting network

Since I left corporate life in 1998, I have been busy solving problems just like Valerie's for companies around the world. I do no advertising outside of the website. Word of mouth and reputation leads to new customers. I've said that if every person who has Excel were aware of what could be done with VBA, there would be enough work to keep an army of MrExcel Consultants busy. I am letting you in on the secret because I am happy to report that we have the army built. Our staff of consultants includes some of the best VBA programmers in the world. They know how to unleash not only the power of Excel, but also to develop world-class solutions for Access, Word, Power Point, Outlook, Visio, and Map Point.

Our consultants and our clients span the globe. Often, we can provide a consultant that speaks your language, literally and figuratively. If our project manager doesn't understand the details, you are put in direct contact with the consultant that is best suited to complete your project.

Our prices suit your needs; we provide consultants at different levels of skills. Why use a VB programmer when all you need is help with a difficult function? Using this method, we provide the most cost-effective solution for you.

Whether you're a VBA Programmer or someone with expert skills in a Microsoft Office application, or a user that needs help with your project, the MrExcel.com Consulting Network has the answer for you!

Yes, We Have No Bananas

I have had the unusual experience of working in an MIS department for a few years and then jumping the fence to join the "user" departments for ten years. I witnessed an amazing phenomenon: "the rise of the Yes, We Have No Bananas" computer programmer.

Growing up, we had an old player piano with a lot of music rolls from the 1920's. As kids, one of our favorite silly songs was "Yes, We Have No Bananas". It was about three Greek brothers – Pete, Nick, and Jim – who ran a fruit store on the street. Any time you asked them for anything, they would never say No. They would just "Yes" you to death and then sell you something else. You would ask for walnuts and they would give you coconuts or, maybe, doughnuts.

Many computer programmers today are very much like Pete, Nick, and Jim. I've sat in meetings between the MIS department and the user department and watched it happen. The accountants ask for a program that will provide XYZ. Programmers are a smart breed. In a few seconds, we can start to program that in our head, realize the hard parts, figure the easy workaround, and then repeat the request back to you, but slightly different.

The accountants ask for XYZ and the programmers cheerfully repeat back, "Yes! We can provide you with XZY". Like "Walnuts and Doughnuts", it sounds the same. It may even be 95% of what the Accountant wanted. The accountants, worn down by years of hassles from the MIS department, are happy to hear a "Yes" and they sign off on the project.

"There are two ways to program every project – there is the easy way, and the right way."

-Bill Jelen

Here is the frustrating truth about this situation: The programmer is correct – providing XZY instead of XYZ will probably shave an hour of development time from the project. (*For the accountants reading this book – what would you do? – Method A will take five minutes to code, and Method B will take an hour and five minutes to code.*) You can't blame the programmer – he is saving you money. The MIS department already has a six-month backlog and their job is to get this done as soon as possible.

"The difference between the right code and almost the right code is like the difference between lightning and the lightning bug."

-Mark Twain,
as adapted for the 21st century

But – here lies the problem. The accountant is going to have to use this program every day. Because the programmer provided a solution that was done the easy way instead of the right way, the accountant will experience three extra mouse clicks per journal entry. Let's say that is 30 seconds per transaction, times 40 transactions a day, times 250 days per year. The programmer saved himself an hour – one time – but is forcing the accountant to waste 10 minutes a day, every day for the next five years. One hour of a programmer's time would have shaved 220 hours of an accountant's time over the five-year period.

This same scenario happens every day in every meeting between the MIS department and the user departments across the world. At the very least, you should hit your MIS director over the head with this book, preferably opened to this page.

It is easy to still want to program the easy way instead of the right way. There is a sign on the wall above my computer that says, "Do it the RIGHT way, not the easy way." I've been there. I've lived on both sides of the fence. Living on the user side of the fence for years should be part of the training regimen for every programmer. Let that programmer do the three extra mouse clicks 200 times a week and watch how fast he would be willing to spend the extra hour to program it the right way. I impart this belief to my project managers and coders.

Coming attractions

After finishing this book, I wrote a follow-up book that was to be titled Programming Excel from the Ground Up - a book for non-programmers. I am pleased to announce that in 2004, the book was published by QUE with the title "VBA and Macros for Microsoft Excel". Although it has a new title, it still meets the original intent. Tracy Syrstad and I walk you through recording a macro, explain why the macro recorder doesn't work, and then show you how to change recorded macros into real macros. The book is available at booksellers everywhere or from MrExcel.com.

I encourage you to send your comments and critiques of this book to me personally at bill@MrExcel.com. I cannot promise to respond to every e-mail I receive, but I will try my best!

-Bill Jelen

HOLY MACRO! BOOKS QUICK ORDER FORM

Fax Orders: (707)-220-4510. Send this form.

E-Mail Orders: store@MrExcel.com - Online: http://www.MrExcel.com

Postal Orders: MrExcel, 13386 Judy Ave NW, Uniontown OH 44685, USA

Quantity	Title	Price	Total
	Holy Macro! It's 2,200 Excel VBA Examples (CD-ROM) By Hans Herber Bill Jelen and Tom Urtis ISBN 1-932802-08-8 (2200 pages – 2004)	$89.00	
	Slide Your Way Through Excel VBA (CD-ROM) By Dr. Gerard Verschuuren ISBN 0-9724258-6-1 (734 pages – 2003)	$99.00	
	Join the Excellers League (CD-ROM) By Dr. Gerard Verschuuren ISBN 1-932802-00-2 (1477 pages – 2004)	$99.00	
	Excel for Scientists (CD-ROM) By Dr. Gerard Verschuuren ISBN 0-9724258-8-8 (589 pages – 2004)	$75.00	
	Guerilla Data Analysis Using Microsoft Excel By Bill Jelen ISBN 0-9724258-0-2 (138 pages – 2002)	$19.95	
	Learn Excel from Mr Excel By Bill Jelen ISBN 1-932802-12-6 (853 pages – 2005)	$39.95	
	The Spreadsheet at 25 By Bill Jelen ISBN 1-932802-04-5 (120 color pages – 2005)	$19.95	
	Grover Park George On Access By George Hepworth ISBN 0-9724258-9-6 (480 pages 2004)	$29.95	
	Your Access to the World (CD-ROM) By Dr. Gerard Verschuuren ISBN 1-932802-03-7 (1450 pages – 2004)	$99.00	
	Access VBA Made Accessible (CD-ROM) By Dr. Gerard Verschuuren (1323 pages – 2004)	$99.00	
	DreamBoat On Word By Anne Troy ISBN 0-9724258-4-5 (220 pages 2004)	$19.95	
	Kathy Jacobs On PowerPoint By Kathy Jacobs ISBN 0-9724258-6-1 (380 pages 2004)	$29.95	
	Unleash the Power of Outlook 2003 By Steve Link ISBN 1-932802-01-0 (250 pages 2004)	$19.95	
	Unleash the Power of OneNote By Kathy Jacobs & Bill Jelen (320 pages, 2004)	$19.95	
	VBA and Macros for Microsoft Excel By Bill Jelen and Tracy Syrstad ISBN 0789731290 (576 Pages 2004)	$39.95	
	Pivot Table Data Crunching By Bill Jelen and Michael Alexander ISBN 0789734354 (275 Pages 2005)	$29.95	

Name: _____

Address: _____

City, State, Zip: _____

E-Mail: _____

Sales Tax: Ohio residents add 6% sales tax

Shipping by Air: **US** $4 for first book, $2 per additional book. $1 per CD.

        International: $9 for first book, $5 per additional book. $2 per CD

        FedEx available on request at actual shipping cost.

Payment: Check or Money order to "MrExcel" or pay with VISA/MC/American Express:

        Card #:_____ Exp.:_____

        Name on Card: _____

Bulk Orders: Ordering enough for the entire accounting staff? Save 40% when you order 6 or more of any one title.